The Author

MADELINE D. INGRAM is widely known for her work throughout the United States with children and youth choirs. She has conducted choir festivals and workshops in more than twenty different states since 1946. Her experience with young people includes a long period as Minister of Music at Memorial Methodist Church in Lynchburg, Virginia, and eight years as a public school teacher in Ohio and North Carolina.

Mrs. Ingram is chairman of the division of fine arts and associate professor of music at Lynchburg College. She is also on the faculty at the Presbyterian School of Christian Education in Richmond.

She has written two earlier books, *Organizing and Directing Children's Choirs* and *Vocal Technique for Children and Youth* both published by Abingdon Press. The latter book she coauthored with William Rice. She is a member of the American Guild of Organists, Hymn Society of America, and Music Educators National Conference.

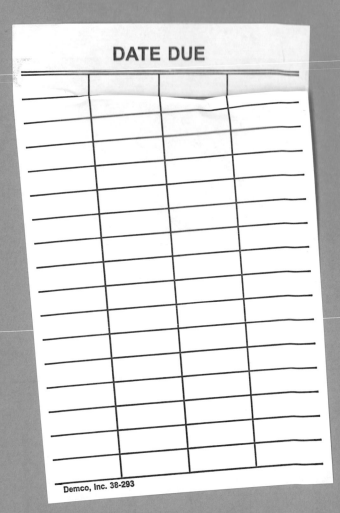

DATE DUE

Demco, Inc. 38-293

A Guide for Youth Choirs

A Guide for Youth Choirs

Madeline D. Ingram

♪

ABINGDON PRESS

Nashville   *New York*

To My Husband

with gratitude for his encouragement and
interest in my choir work

Contents

1

Why Youth Choirs?

"Why are there so few young people in our Sunday morning services?" This question is all too frequently asked in countless churches across the country. Take a good look at churches you know and see whether or not this is a valid question. Now take a look at the church school classes and the Sunday evening youth fellowship group and you will probably be surprised at the number of young folk you see there. Why is it that so many of them go home after church school instead of remaining for the church service?

Is it because the service does not interest and challenge them? Is it because they have not had sufficient instruction in understanding the elements of worship in their church and find them meaningless? Is it because the hymn singing is so dull and half-hearted that they feel no desire to join in? Is it because they feel that nothing is required of them? Of course, all the congregation is expected to participate in hymn singing, responsive reading, and other responsorial parts of the service, but are these things urgently required—even demanded—of them? Do young people feel any special inclination to lift their voices when those around them are often mute? Youth is restless; it wants to feel, to experience, to act.

Opportunities for specific action in the Sunday morning service are few. Only two offer themselves to laymen—ushering and singing in a choir. Ushers are usually members of the governing body of the local church. Because of age and lack of experience young people are incompetent to serve in this body. What of the choir? Except in small churches where there is a paucity of singers, the "regular" choir is made up of older people with more mature voices. Strange as it may seem, there are a surprising number of churches in which the adults do not want young people in their choir and will actually make them feel unwanted and unwelcome. Even in churches where they are accepted into the adult choir, they seldom feel that they really belong to the group, but are merely outsiders.

Attendance at a Sunday evening youth fellowship meeting will show you different young people than those who sit passively in church on Sunday morning. Here there is action, here there is enthusiastic participation, here youth has a place for itself and is happy. Listen to them sing! Are these the same young people who, if they were at morning service, sat dumbly in the pews?

Lucky the youth whose church is now making provision for their energies to find an outlet in service to the church, and in intellectual and emotional benefit to themselves. Young people's choirs are now being given a place of prominence in the musical and educational program offered by churches, and their growing number testifies to their success. That young people have so frequently demanded a choir of their own is also proof of the success of such a program.

Choirs for young people—youth choirs—are more recent in practice than choirs for children. Perhaps they are a natural outgrowth of children's choirs, for as young children advance in age they want their choir experiences to continue, but do not want to stay in a group with younger children. The shared interests and activities of youth, even their own special language, set them apart from those older and younger. Those days when "junior" choirs were made up of youngsters of an approximate age range of nine to sixteen are about over, for we now know that the learning experience is best developed when shared with those of comparable age.

Beside the enjoyment young people find in a choir of their own, there are many other valuable benefits to them. Choristers in any choir have the responsibility, along with the minister, of being leaders in worship. This means that they will have to learn much about worship, both personal and corporate, and its pattern in their church. Intelligence about the meaning and practice of worship makes for keen interest in the service of worship, and this interest makes a strong leader. Responsibility for musical portions of the service such as hymn singing, anthem singing, sung responses; for spoken portions such as responsive reading, prayers, spoken responses; and right attitudes of worship—all are required of choir members.

As choirs sing repeatedly in services in the church and community the members gain confidence in themselves and hence become more competent leaders. Poise, that elusive quality that must be earned, comes with repeated practice in appearing before others. Shyness is natural to many young people who have not yet achieved enough maturity to feel secure. Group activities help these people by making them feel important and by causing them to appear frequently before the public.

Group experiences also help them learn to make satisfactory adjustments to others of their own age, whether of the same or opposite sex. Music proves to be a good stabilizer of the emotions for those whose emotions are becoming increasingly perceptive.

Self-discipline is learned and practiced in a choir. Each member must learn to perform his functions in balance with those of his fellow members. He must sing neither too loud nor too soft; he must learn his part well; he must be regular in attendance at rehearsals and church services; and he is responsible for the neatness of his appearance when vested.

Youth choir members are given the opportunity to learn to use both their singing and speaking voices properly. Weekly vocal instruction is most necessary to them during the time when their voices need careful watching. They are given free voice lessons and at the same time they receive emotional and mental stimulation through singing good music.

These choir members acquire a knowledge of church music such as they would never learn elsewhere. Since they are open-minded and not yet definitely set in their likes and dislikes, they enjoy learning music of all periods. Much of the glorious music of the early days of the church is little sung today, but educated musicians, even young ones, find in it deep satisfaction and rare beauty. Because they like it they sing it convincingly. Contemporary music, the music of their time, is also enthusiastically learned. In fact, the whole gamut of church music can be opened to them with full assurance of its warm reception. Hymn study must receive their attention. No choir member is worthy of the name unless he knows and respects the hymns of the church. In the choir he will be constantly rehearsing and studying them. This cannot help but engender interest in and fondness for them.

Great religious verse makes up the texts of worthy church music, and only this kind should be presented to young people in a church choir. They have plenty of opportunity to hear sentimental "religious" twaddle elsewhere, unfortunately! When superior texts are matched with superior music, they leave a significant mark on those who learn them. Biblical texts, or those inspired by the Bible, if so treated, have fresh meaning for the singer. He cannot sing such texts repeatedly without having their imprint upon him.

Youth itself is not the only group to derive benefit from a choir program. The church reaps many benefits, also. The first is that it receives the inspiration of hearing beautiful music expressively sung by youth. This is a high point in any service. Young voices have a vital freshness which makes what they sing especially beautiful. Because of this, it is often the case that their singing speaks more directly to

14

the listener than what is sung by more mature voices.

Second, the church is constantly developing educated leadership among those who will eventually be in leadership capacity. Loyalty to a church comes very largely through service to it, and this service is best started at an early age. Many years of observation of people who began serving the church through its children's and youth choirs have convinced me of the value of this practice of giving early active support to the church.

Third, congregational participation in church services will be greatly stimulated through the prepared leadership of the choir. Choirs are usually visible to a congregation, and to see one that is obviously enjoying hymn singing and is intelligently reading the responses tends to infect others.

Fourth, although many teen-age choristers are already members of the church, choir membership will tend to influence those who are not members to affiliate with the church. Interest in the church grows as one serves it, and a desire for a closer connection with it develops. A choir that has a reputation for excellence will attract young people who are not members of another church. Whole families are often brought into a church through the interest of one of its members in a choir.

Fifth, a church with a youth choir is growing a

congregation that is more devout. This is brought about by the informed, vigorous participation of its younger members. Its congregations of the future will surely worship in spirit.

Sixth, a capable, dedicated choir is an asset to any church. To have another choir in addition to the adult group that is as capable of fulfilling all the duties of leadership in the church service is cause for pride.

There was a time when it was thought that one of the most important reasons for having a youth choir was to train singers for the adult choir, and this is still a worthy reason. It is foolish to expect, however, that every person who is now a teen-ager will remain forever in his home church. Young people have a way of growing up and going away to college, or marrying and leaving for another city. Although this is a loss to the home church, it is not a cause for frustration. Churches make happy exchanges, gaining new members as old ones leave. It is more and more likely these days that the new members will be people who have had the benefit of choir training and who will want to continue to be of service in a choir. Looking at it in another way, we can say that the church that sends well-trained choristers into other communities is making a valuable contribution to Christianity. The onetime teen-agers who remain in their home church but who drop out of choirs for a good and valid reason (and it is unlikely that they will drop out for any other) will still be of great value as members of the congregation. Nothing is lost.

Through a youth choir program the church benefits, the choristers benefit, the program of Christian education benefits, and the cause of Christianity benefits.

2

The Director

The director of a youth choir needs the same qualifications that are necessary for the successful direction of any other choir, plus one more characteristic—genuine interest in young people. In dealing with adolescents he will need patience, knowledge of their vocal problems, understanding of their emotional needs, and genuine appreciation of them. He should have a sincere respect for them as interesting people, rather than regarding them as vexatious problems.

Adolescence, that time when boys are becoming

18

men and girls are becoming women, is as difficult a time for them as it is for those who must deal with them. Knowledge of what can be expected of them, what traits are common to each sex, what is happening to them emotionally, psychologically, and physically is needed by the person who is to teach them. It is highly desirable for their choir director to be able to give them counsel and help with their problems, big and small.

So much has been said about the difficulties of working with teen-agers that many people are discouraged before they make their acquaintance and find how delightful they can be.

Federal Lee Whittlesey says in his book *A Comprehensive Program of Church Music* that "the music in a church mirrors its director." As we consider this statement, each of us can take a quick survey of the music in churches of his acquaintance and evaluate Dr. Whittlesey's statement in the light of our findings. What kind of director is betokened when a choir sings poorly, when its attire is disheveled, when it is inattentive to all parts of the service except those with which it is directly concerned? Is theirs the director who never plans his rehearsals but bumbles through them, good-naturedly allowing the choristers to dictate their manner of singing and even the kind of music to be sung? Is he the person who believes that if he is not hard on people they will like him better? Does he do the same humdrum things at each rehearsal, leaving his choristers neither inspired nor challenged?

Although no choir leader is perfect, he should constantly strive to improve his fitness for the task. It is hoped and expected that he will have musical ability and teaching skills sufficient to translate his learning to others. A knowledge of vocal techniques will stand him in good stead, but he will also need to learn a great deal about the special vocal problems that confront the adolescent. Methods of handling such problems have changed in recent years, but books and magazines that deal with the new trends are available to all.

A harmonious relation with the director of choral music in the high school is most desirable. Both directors are teaching many of the same people and working on the same vocal problems with them. The task of selecting suitable music for use with these groups is mutual also, and it is possible that the schoolteacher receives more catalogs and advertising than are sent to a church. High schoolers have been heard to complain that the music offered them at church did not compare with what they sang at school, and was of little interest to them. The church director should try to hear school concerts sung by these people, for it will help him to listen to them objectively as well as give him an insight into the type of music they are capable of singing. His presence at concerts will also show the young people that his interest in them lies outside as well as inside the church.

Because his work with music is in a church, a choir director serves as a religious guide to youth as well as a musical guide. The days of youth are sometimes difficult, as childhood beliefs are developing into those of an adult. Elizabeth Hurlock, in her book *Adolescent Development,* says, "Because religion is so strong a factor in producing security, the adolescent should have the type of religious belief that can stand the strain of adolescent conflict and doubt—few religious beliefs acquired in childhood have the qualities the youth needs. For that reason, some revision must be made before his former religious beliefs can prove satisfactory."

Because adolescence is a time of emotional awakening, youth develops a sensitivity to the arts. All these, but especially music, can play a large part in helping teen-agers find a renewed and expanded interest in religion.

It is, of course, self-evident that the director himself should be a practicing Christian, and that his example should earn him the respect of young people. The group with which he is dealing is highly impressionable, and they may catch more from his actions than his spoken words.

Young people in choir are not the only ones with whom the director will come in contact. Much of the success of any church music program depends upon the interest and goodwill of people outside the immediate program. Some church musicians show a lack of interest in other branches of church work than their own, and this is an unforgivable fault. It is only natural that the leaders in each branch of Christian education, being engrossed in their special areas, tend to look upon their own more favorably than another, but it must be remembered that only when all areas work harmoniously together are desired goals realized. Besides the minister and other youth leaders, many people other than choir members are interested in music and will surely call upon the choir director to give time and energy to them. He may be asked to speak to groups of various ages, he may be called upon to provide music for a weekday meeting; he may be asked to present his choir at a community meeting; and he may be called upon to direct music festivals locally or abroad. All these involve him with many types of people. Tact, genuine goodwill, and interest in the cause of church music will give him status in the church and community.

It is to be expected that a choir director will have the ability to communicate with his choir, but he will be called upon to address other groups in the church in both speech and writing. Members of a church are entitled to know what the choir director is doing and what he hopes to do. The governing body of the church has the right to question a director about his work, and they will likely ask for a personal appearance when he is applying for the position. The too glib, the too reticent person is not as well received as the one who is politely at ease and who can present his facts clearly and concisely. Ease in public speaking comes for most people with practice, and the director should welcome every opportunity to improve his abilities. Good posture, good diction, and good speech organization will insure that the speaker will be listened to.

The choir director will often have to write material for the church bulletin, the church papers, and sometimes for the city paper. Such writing should be terse, succinct, and pithy. It must cause the reader to want to read it. He will do well to study magazine and newspaper advertising so as to imitate some of the eye-catching ideas displayed there. These may be used in poster-making or writing newspaper advertisements.

Information presented in a Sunday church bulletin about the music to be used in the service can be very dull reading. "The music of the anthem sung by the youth choir was composed by Austin Lovelace, Minister of Music at the Montview Boulevard Presbyterian Church, Denver, Colorado," will create no interest in the listener. "Austin Lovelace, a contemporary composer of church music, delights in delving into old hymnals, pulling out currently little-known tunes, and arranging them for present-day usage. Such an anthem is the one sung by the youth choir today. Notice its folklike simplicity and sincerity." This channels the listening interest of the congregation. The same tactics should be used with hymns. A few words to pique the interest and make the hymn more than a casual routine pay dividends.

To be of most value to the church and its choristers, the director should learn as much as possible about it and its tenets. A director who has had long association with a Presbyterian church and who goes to work in a Methodist church must learn what differences there are in creeds, organization, theology, and teaching practices. He need not necessarily become a member of the church he is serving, though this is thought by most people to be desirable, but he must abide by and honor its practices while there. In changing from one denomination to another, he must often confer with the minister and others who are in a leadership capacity. He must become familiar with the hymnal, the prayer book, and the teaching materials for the church school. Practices and customs within the local church as well as those of the denomination must be recognized also, for in most denominations the local church is given considerable freedom of movement. To lead people in a religious faith demands that the leader know that faith.

The dedicated director will give so much time and energy to his work that at the end of a nine- or ten-month season he often feels completely drained and in need of restoration. He also feels the need of new materials and ideas. This is the time for him to go to a summer conference on church music. The choice is great, for all across the country there are such gatherings, lasting from a few days to two weeks, and dealing with both specific and general aspects of music in the church. At these conferences directors share ideas, sit in classes taught by skilled leaders, play instruments, listen to concerts, sing, enjoy good fellowship, and come out rejuvenated. Music displays are there for their perusal, and these are of particular benefit to the directors in smaller towns where there are no music stores. There are three widely circulated magazines that carry frequent articles about youth choirs, and that often include anthems suitable for them. These are: *Music Ministry, The Church Musician, The Youth Musician,* and *Journal of Church Music.* In each of these, articles and usable suggestions are written by knowledgeable people in the field of church music and are a source of valuable help.

Diapason, issued monthly by the American Guild of Organists, carries occasional articles about young choirs, although these are not always in the form of practical helps.

An organization that devotes itself entirely to young choirs is the Choristers Guild. From its headquarters at 440 Northlake Center, Dallas, Texas, it issues monthly "Letters" that abound with all manner of helps for the director. This organization serves experienced as well as amateur directors and is considered invaluable by all of them. Besides the information it dispenses in the "Letters," it encourages its members to send in questions and requests for specific help. It also sponsors one or more annual seminars where professional and amateur directors meet for one week and profit by association with one another, by listening to lectures, and by seeing demonstration rehearsals. In some areas there are local chapters of the Choristers Guild in which all directors of youth choirs are eligible for membership.

Other workshops are held throughout the country, sponsored by local churches, American Guild of Organists, or denominational groups, and most of these include at least one course for directors of youth choirs. Even those that are sponsored by a given denomination do not exclude members of others, and the lectures and demonstrations presented are valuable to all.

One of the gratifying characteristics of most church musicians is their willingness to help others and to share their ideas and findings. Any amateur director should feel free to call for help from anyone who is engaged in like work. Not only will this be flattering to those of more experience, but more frequently than not they will be sincerely eager to help in the development of a program in which they believe.

THE DIRECTOR

It is one thing to have the inspiration of a summer conference, but that is really not enough. The learning process must go on perpetually. There is opportunity in many towns to continue study in colleges, and in others there are extension courses. Many a director who has had no time previously for courses that interest him is stimulated by taking advantage of such study now. There is education also in playing in a small ensemble, joining a group of recorder players, or singing in a community chorus. This may be the time to learn to play the viola or the piccolo or to study speech. The wise director tries to budget his time so that it is possible for him always to have the stimulation of studying something.

Directing a youth choir program is no job for a lethargic person. Keeping up with the activities of young people is a job in itself. Attendance at school concerts, plays, athletic events, as well as similar activities within the church, is highly desirable for the director—yes, even necessary. Conducting rehearsals so that they are always challenging and interesting takes energy and enthusiasm. Unless a director is excited about what he is doing, he cannot expect others to be. Enthusiasm is like measles, easily caught!

We have consistently referred to the director as "he," but this is not to indicate that "she" cannot do the job as well. It is not so much the sex of the director of youth choirs as it is personality and ability to communicate with young people that distinguishes the good from the mediocre. Young people must not only like but have respect for their choir director, and it is incumbent upon those of us who are directors to earn this respect.

3

Organizing the Youth Choir

Multiple choir programs are popular, and with good reason. They provide choir experiences for people of comparable ages and interests. They offer a progressive education in church music, for each will continue the learning begun in the preceding choir.

Some of the most successful choirs are those whose members have grown into a youth choir from well-directed younger choirs. In those choirs they will have learned many valuable things: to sing well, to take their place in a worship service, to love the music of the church, and to achieve the necessary disciplines and responsibilities.

If a church has such a choir program, there is little or no difficulty in organizing and maintaining a youth choir. Once he is in a stimulating choir program, a chorister rarely wants to depart from it. He will automatically go from one choir to another as his age increases, and he is not likely to remark that he believes he will "give up choir."

With sufficient time and patience many directors in churches where a multiple choir program is being developed will build new choirs as the need for them arises. Thus primary choristers will move into a junior choir, and they in turn will progress to a junior high choir and later into one made up of senior highs. This is an ideal method of establishing a youth choir—letting the need for it grow out of previous experiences.

If, however, a church wants to establish immediately a choir or choirs for youth, it must think of ways to launch the project successfully. First the church must ask itself some questions:

1. Does it have adequate leadership?

2. Are there enough young people to warrant the success of the undertaking?

3. Can it financially afford another choir?

4. Will it support the choir with genuine interest?

Organizing the Youth Choir

There is no plan of action that will work equally well for all churches. Much depends upon the director, the number and personalities of the young people, and the active support of the church and its minister. The latter carries far more influence in this matter than is sometimes realized. His approval of a choir and his proper support of it will generate interest and commendation among members of the church. In order to give this support he must be fully aware of the aims and goals and potentials of the choir. Choir directors are often guilty of failure to discuss choir plans with their ministers, and then they wonder why ministers are not more cooperative and sympathetic in music matters. Other people with whom the choir director must work closely are the director of Christian education and the leader of the youth fellowship group. Integration of activities is a necessity. Music in the church is a part of the whole religious experience of youth, not just one facet set apart, and it is most important to remember this.

Youth choirs have been successfully developed out of a Sunday evening youth program. Young people clearly show that they enjoy singing together at these meetings, and if the choir director leads such singing, he will have an opportunity to become acquainted with the group. Fellowship songs have a tendency to relax the singers and put them at ease. A skilled director can make them enjoy hymns, rounds, and even easy anthems. Observation will

31

show that when songs are sung by rote nearly everyone joins in, but that when the young people are given music to read there is a distinct quieting down. Can the director sneak in a little session of note reading and still not lose the interest of the singers? Yes, indeed, it can be done and has been done!

One youth choir was started by an aspiring director's interest in a Hebrew benediction that she overheard some of the young people singing informally. When she asked where they learned it, they replied that one of the college boys had taught it to them in their Sunday evening fellowship meeting. When she asked if she might meet with them the following Sunday in order to learn it, she was enthusiastically welcomed. At that meeting one of the singers asked her a question about Hebrew music, and she at once not only answered the question but showed them the Hebrew tunes in their hymnal and offered to bring a recording of Hebrew music to their next meeting if they so desired. From that chance beginning a church music study was begun which led into the formation of a youth choir.

Most young people are interested in languages and are studying them at school. Presenting music as another language and not a thing that is abstract, remote, impossibly difficult to learn, makes for a desire to learn to read it. Let no one feel that his inability to read music is a formidable barrier over which he cannot climb without laborious toiling and moiling. There are books which will aid the director in presenting this elementary material to youth in a manner that will attract them. One such is Howard Shanet's *Learn to Read Music*. The Sunday evening singing time may well lead into a desire for more instruction and more singing experiences, and thus the formation of a choir results.

Another method of organizing a youth choir is to send out calls for members. Unless the young people who are popular with the others are interested, the rest of the group is unlikely to respond, or will respond in such small numbers as to insure the failure of the project. Interest the group leaders first, and through them build a choir.

Christmas pageants are universally popular, and they involve people of many ages. One youth choir was the outgrowth of such a pageant. The church's director of music was responsible for its presentation, and at the same time he was eager to organize a youth choir. He asked two very popular boys and three such girls to be cantors in the pageant. Then he "found" he needed a singing group, and asked these popular folk to help him get such a group together. He saw to it that the song material was easy but stimulating, and he called for extra rehearsals with them, always including his popular quintet. To his delight, one of the group suggested that since they were having such a good time together it seemed a pity to stop when the pageant was finished. Gradually, and tactfully, more and more young people were added to the group, and it developed into a very fine choir that served its community as well as its church.

Personal contact is absolutely essential. Visits to him in his home give an opportunity for good appraisal of a youth's personality. Be sure to select an appropriate time for calling, for if your visit interferes with something already planned by the young person, his annoyance may make him rebellious toward you and your project.

Follow the personal visit by mailing a notice that is attractive and informative. It should make the recipient feel needed and wanted. It should announce the first meeting of the group and contain any other pertinent information.

Some sample letters such as these may be used:

You Are Wanted

By whom?   Your church music program

Why?   Because you have something valuable to give

Where?   In the Youth Choir

When?   Now

First Rehearsal

September 22
Church Music Room
4:00-5:00

Epworth Methodist Church   Meeting House Lane

ORGANIZING THE YOUTH CHOIR

We Are Looking for You

At

Our First Choir Rehearsal

On

Wednesday, September 20

4:00-5:00

To

Learn of the exciting events planned
for this year
Elect officers
Start learning our new music

In

The Music Room

First Presbyterian Church   First and Grove Streets

Talking to young people in church school and
youth meetings, placing alluring posters at strategic
spots in the education building, making announce-
ments in the church bulletin and newspaper are
all effective. Notices in local newspapers often attract youth who are not already attending any
church but who like to sing with others their age.

One of the things that will spell sure disaster to
the undertaking of choir organization is to contact
the young people through their parents, for now, as
at no other time in their lives, they want to feel
capable of making their own decisions. A young
person who is made to come to choir is of no value

to the organization, and he will receive little benefit to himself.

It is always hard to find a choir rehearsal time that is equally convenient and agreeable to all young people concerned. High school athletics are popular and are entered into by many boys and girls. Practice time for team sports is often scheduled after class hours. Dramatics are popular also, and play rehearsals occupy many after school hours. Some high school music groups such as band and orchestra frequently rehearse in late afternoon. Parents usually require their children to be at home on school nights, and weekend nights are the time for ball games and parties.

In churches where there is a midweek family night program it is possible to schedule a youth choir rehearsal in early evening of that day. The time that appears to be most generally popular, however, is Sunday afternoon before the fellowship supper and meeting. This makes it ideally a part of the Christian education program, and planning it in conjunction with the rest of the youth program may attract more young people. If there are separate choirs for junior highs and senior highs, the director will need an assistant, or he must adjust the rehearsal schedule accordingly.

Once the choir is formed, the young people may want to organize it, for they love clubs and organizations of all kinds. Officers might well be president, secretary, librarian, and if they feel the need for one, treasurer. The president will preside at all business meetings of the group and work closely with the director in all matters pertaining to the welfare of the choir. The secretary will be responsible for roll taking and the sending of notices, cards to members who are ill, and so on. The librarian will be responsible for the care, distribution, and collection of the music and hymnals. Whether or not a choir treasurer is needed depends upon the wishes of the choir. If they want to engage in activities such as trips and parties where extra funds are needed, they may want to accumulate money for such purposes. They may amass such a reserve by contributions, moneymaking projects (if the church allows it), and/or choir dues. If dues are required, they should be for a very small amount so that no one is eliminated because of them.

Choir funds can be used to pay for any correspondence necessary to the groups, for providing altar flowers at least once a year, and to help pay for an occasional party or outing. Certainly no choir is a social club, but it is necessary for young people to have fun times together, and these funds will help to defray expenses. Young people seem to be full of ideas for moneymaking, but they should be guided in this by their director.

What age divisions should be made in youth choirs? It depends largely upon the community. In a small town where all the people know each other and where young people are attending school in the same building, the choir age limits are broad. In such a situation there may not be enough young people in a single church to form more than one group. But in a city, where there is much rivalry between the junior and senior high schools, there is usually a marked lack of compatibility between youth who are placed together. This need not be so, of course, but in far too many situations it has been the cause of limited choir benefits. The age limits of choirs may be determined by having them coincide with church school departments. This would mean that there would be an intermediate choir that might not be made up entirely of junior high youngsters. The high school group, however, will be likely to consist of those who are in one of the three or four grades of high school.

Should there be separate choirs for boys and girls of junior high age? Boys' voices make for problems by the time they reach this age, and many directors feel that both they and the girls profit by having their own choirs.

Because of the unreliable state of the boys' voices, they cannot all sing the same parts. Some of them will still be singing a good, clear soprano while others begin to show a reedy, husky quality. A boy choir answers many problems for boys and their director. I have had such a choir for many years, and believe it is highly beneficial to both sexes.

There were no dropouts among the boys, all of them remaining in choir throughout the entire period of voice change.

Boys of junior age—nine, ten, eleven—and boys of intermediate age—twelve, thirteen, fourteen—combine well.

When I first planned to try such an age grouping for boys, I feared that the older boys might feel so superior to the younger ones that the mixture might not be feasible. I devised a "buddy" program that not only worked well at the start but has continued to work. Each older boy has a younger one as a "buddy" for whom he is responsible. He sits with him in his first rehearsals, he helps him with his vestment and hymnal on Sunday, and he is responsible for him in every way. This makes the older fellows feel needed and important, and they bask in the admiration of the younger boys, while the little fellows in turn are flattered at the attention of those who are older. We cannot definitely say that at fourteen a boy will automatically go on into another choir, for much will depend upon the condition of his voice at that time, but we can expect that he will be ready to move on.

In a group of boys no one feels embarrassed if his voice does not properly respond to his will. If girls are present, however, boys are ill at ease when this happens, and they all too frequently drop out of choir rather than appear to disadvantage before the girls. In an all-boy group frank discussion of vocal problems and their treatment creates interest in the situation for those whose voices are changing and for those who are approaching this state. Each individual voice is a subject of concern to the group, and as they follow its progress with profit to themselves, the changing voice becomes a subject of importance. A by-product of this kind of treatment is the interest the younger boys take in the development of the older voices. This may seem trivial, but it does make for a good climate, for the older boys love to be looked up to and made to feel important. Younger boys often have their favorites, and rivalry ensues over which voice is making the most progress toward maturity. Isn't this much better than letting the boys with changing voices feel shame and chagrin?

If such a choir is made available for boys, what do we do with the girls? They must have a choir of their own, too. For some peculiar reason girls of ages nine to fourteen do not combine satisfactorily. The older girls feel very much aloof and have an unfortunate inclination to look down on those who are younger. Junior girls work well together, and even twelve-year-olds may successfully be added to the group. This leaves the thirteen- and fourteen-year-olds in a separate choir to which most directors add the twelve-year-olds. As will be discussed in a later chapter, the girls have some vocal problems as they reach early teens, and in a choir of their own more time can be given to them.

Each church and each director must work out choir groupings according to the available choristers, the use the choir will be put to, possible rehearsal schedules, and the director's schedule.

4

The Rehearsal

No good choir is the result of indifferent rehearsals. Such rehearsals are always the fault of the director. The flurried person who arrives at the church with the choristers can expect an apathetic session from which both he and the singers emerge tired and with little or nothing accomplished. The person who has made no lesson plan for a rehearsal but who expects to "play it by ear" will reap the same frustration. So will the director who looks forward with dread to an hour of trying to cope with teen-agers.

To be successful the director must approach the rehearsals with enthusiasm and well-laid plans. He must design his work so as to provide stimulating, satisfying experiences for the singers, and for himself. He must have long-range plans as well as weekly ones.

In making long-range plans he must:

1. Keep in mind the musical growth he wants for his choristers. No earnest director wants his choir to reach a point of musical accomplishment and knowledge and remain forever at that point. Choristers need the stimulation of continuous schooling in the mechanics of music making. Choir training should be a perpetual music education, meeting the needs and aptitudes of each age level.

2. Remember the necessity for variety in materials. Young people are restless and in need of variety in all things. If their interest in choir music is to be maintained, it must be energized with challenging and interesting song material. Many a young person has become bored with choir because he was asked consistently to sing music that was insipid and monotonous.

3. Plan for times when the choir will sing an anthem in Sunday services. Choirs must sing in services frequently if their interest is to be upheld. Minister and choir director need to plan together for all services so that the director may properly prepare for a suitable choir to lead in each. This must be scheduled far in advance if the choir is to

make a satisfactory contribution to the service. A calendar indicating the choir or choirs to provide anthems for each service should be prepared several months in advance. A September-January schedule should be planned before the choir season starts in the fall, and the February-June schedule should be set up by mid-December.

4. Plan for musical services in which the choirs will play an important part or for which they are entirely responsible. Occasions when each choir sings in festivals, in combination with other choirs, or in services other than those regularly scheduled must be entered on the choir calendar, too. This enables choristers to keep the dates open for these activities, and it insures ample time for adequate preparation. These extra times should be spaced over fairly wide intervals, of course.

5. Select materials to be used in connection with other choirs. Finding just the right anthems to be sung by combined choirs takes time. There is a reasonably wide variety on the market, but not all of them suit every choir. Consideration must be given to the vocal abilities of the groups involved, the number of singers in each group, and the use for which the material is intended. It is perhaps safe to say that there is more available material for the Christmas season than any other, but we must not confine combined choir singing to that season alone.

44

Many anthems not already so indicated can be made suitable for use by more than one choir if the director uses his imagination.

Solo parts may be sung by an entire group rather than an individual; descants may be sung by a children's choir or by high school girls; and even four-part sections may be sung in unison, if desired.

6. Learn thoroughly all voice parts of the music he expects to teach. How can a director be certain when one voice part sings a wrong note, or even when one singer sings a wrong note, unless he knows each part thoroughly himself? Advance preparation will also alert him as to where difficulties may arise, thus enabling him better to help the singers over such hurdles.

In making weekly plans the director should:

1. Decide which new material is to be introduced and the manner of its presentation.

2. Select review material, planning to work only on the sections that were weak last rehearsal. Using materials that are in varying stages of completion helps to maintain interest.

3. Plan for changes of pace throughout the rehearsal.

4. Make certain he knows each note of every voice part.

5. Practice conducting selections to be worked so that his movements are clear and concise.

6. Obtain a list of hymns to be sung the following

Sunday, and plan the manner of presentation to choir so as to sustain interest.

7. Arrange materials so that successive numbers are not in the same key, rhythm, or mood.

8. Advise the accompanist of all material to be worked.

In preparing for each weekly rehearsal the accompanist should:

1. Practice the accompaniment for each anthem to be used. Learn to play it well. An ill-prepared, stumbling accompanist can wreck any rehearsal.

2. Practice each voice part alone, then in combination with one or more of the other voice parts.

3. Practice the hymns.

4. Practice responses, if any.

On the day of the rehearsal the director should arrive at the rehearsal room in time to:

1. See that hymnals and song materials are conveniently placed and ready in the order of expected use. Valuable time is lost when singers have to thumb through a stack of music to find the one needed. Passing out and collecting each anthem as it is needed is another time waster. Most directors feel that folders for each member are the most efficient means of keeping music ready.

2. Arrange for seating if movable chairs are used. If at all possible, it seems best for singers to rehearse in the same formation they will have in the

church service. Definite seats within a given voice section should be assigned. This may have to change within the year if there are voice changes, of course. All singers must be so placed that they see the director at all times.

3. Provide for the best possible ventilation, remembering that pitch problems arise from overheated rooms.

4. Have chalkboard material ready, if it is to be used.

5. See that the bulletin board is up-to-date, with new notices or clippings only.

6. Have his own music and lesson plans in order.

7. Resolve not to talk too much!

Rehearsals should always start and stop on time. Begin the very first rehearsal of the year at exactly the time set, and end it the same way. Those who are inclined to be laggards soon get the idea. Left to themselves, young people often are lackadaisical about deadlines of time, so the director must establish the precept.

It is too often the case that choirs do not have a room of their own in which to rehearse but must use whatever is available. New churches, recognizing the expanding choir program, are providing proper choir rooms, but there are still more choirs in old buildings than new. If it is possible, select a room that is fairly large and acoustically good (neither too live nor too dead), has seats that promote good posture, can be well ventilated, has windows to the back or side of the singers, and has a piano in good condition.

The necessity for a sizable room is obvious. Since the choir will eventually present its music in a large room, they must learn in rehearsal to project their voices to suit the room. Chairs, provided they have straight backs, are better than benches, since they can be arranged at will. Folding chairs, however, often tilt the singer backward into an incorrect singing position. Singers must always have both feet on the floor, and chairs must help to make this possible and comfortable.

A change of air is necessary to singers, and if the arrangement of the room does not permit fresh air to come in throughout the rehearsal, windows must be thrown open at least once. Singers who must face into bright light coming through windows are blinded by it, so every effort must be made to avoid this.

As has repeatedly been said, church pianos are often among the poorest to be found. If such a one is used in choir rehearsal, just think what it can do to singers who are expected to match its pitches! It is possible, and even desirable, to do much unaccompanied singing, although most groups need piano help, too.

Regular attendance at rehearsals is necessary. Absences must be explained before they occur or as soon thereafter as possible. There must be an understanding as to whether a chorister who misses a rehearsal is permitted to sing with the choir the following Sunday. If a chorister misses for a legitimate reason only one rehearsal prior to the singing of an anthem, is dependable, and knows the music thoroughly, it would seem that he should be allowed to appear with his choir. The policy should be made by the director, for he is responsible for the end results. Whatever rule he makes must be consistently followed.

School activities often compete for the student's time, but if the choir rehearsals bring pleasure and satisfaction, singers will do their best to avoid missing them. In some communities schools and churches work together to allow young people time for activities connected with each. If a choir has made, with the director's help, its attendance requirements, they must be met accordingly. Nothing slipshod is to be tolerated in any part of the choir program.

Rehearsal procedure will vary with the director and with each individual rehearsal. Directors must always remember, though, to keep the rehearsal moving, the choristers busy. They must have time for bodily movement. Standing, sitting, conducting, practicing processionals, doing a few calisthenics are a few ways to shift position profitably.

Each rehearsal should include learning new material, reviewing and polishing old material, singing with and without accompaniment, and vocal drill. Although it will not be done every week, time should frequently be allotted for listening to recorded music.

Some directors start each rehearsal with vocal drill, while others feel that singing should come first with drill following as needed. Alternating procedures is advantageous. If singing does come first, it should involve known or partially known material. If the material is very well known, care must be taken to see that the singing is a real means of getting together vocally rather than a humdrum repetition that accomplishes nothing. Directors who use a familiar hymn as an opener may be guilty of contributing to that vast number of people who think of hymns as a matter of routine singing and nothing more. Unless care is taken to treat the first singing as important, the rehearsal will get off to a slow start.

Work on partially known material usually comes early in a rehearsal. Musicians are frequently guilty of wasting time by going over an entire piece of music when only a few measures are giving difficulty. Since it is easy to forget from one rehearsal to another where difficulties occurred, it is well to mark them at the time they arise so that they are quickly found when lesson plans are being made. If problems arise in one voice part only, the rest of the choir will become bored if too much time is spent correcting the one group. Perhaps they may hum their own parts softly, or, if range permits, everyone may sing the difficult part in unison until the troubled section feels secure.

When reviewing an entire song it is sometimes beneficial to have only a few voices sing it first while the rest listen. Or it may be played through exactly as it is to be sung, the choristers visually following the score. Singing it without accompaniment will prove how well it is learned. Before any music is sung publicly, it must be so well known by the singers that nothing can go wrong in performance. It must be practiced in the place where it will be sung, and with the accompanying instrument that will be used. Many people feel lack of support with an organ in a large room, though they were comfortable with a piano in a small room.

New material should be a challenge to everyone—to the director who must "sell" it to his choir and to the singers who are to learn it. Far too many directors present new material without remembering to whet the singers' appetites first. Motivation may be incited in many ways: by interesting information about the text, the tune, the composer, the author; the circumstance which prompted its writing or composition; an analysis of the music; or the use the choir will make of it. One of these will suffice at a time with perhaps others added in succeeding rehearsals. The challenge of music analysis is entered into enthusiastically by teen-agers, and it speeds up the learning process when they can discover repetitions, rhythmic and key changes by themselves.

Another way to present new material is to let the choir hear it before they attempt to learn it. Hearing the text read expressively so that the thought content is understood is profitable. This will be a later help in using correct diction, dynamics, and phrasing. This may be followed by the group reading it in unison, then in note rhythm. Another way of hearing before singing is to follow the score as the piece is played through. While it is being played a second time, the choristers may hum their parts or sing on a neutral syllable such as ah or loo. If there is a good recording available, the same method may be pursued.

One area of choir singing that is all too often neglected is that of preparation for hymn singing. Since it is the duty of all choirs to help lead the congregation in singing hymns, they should be carefully prepared to give such leadership with strength and intelligence. Keeping his choirs alert and sensitive to oft-repeated hymns is one of the most challenging jobs a director has. Hymns can be made interesting when approached from a variety of angles—history, music, and literature being among those most commonly used. Each time the choir sings them there should be an improvement over the last singing.

A complete study of the hymnal used in one's own church should be made at some time or other.

It is frequently included in the training of a junior choir, but if it has been omitted then it should be taken up by the teen-agers. A systematic study of the development in this area of church music has been known to intrigue young people. Most hymnals carry examples of all types of hymns, from plainsong to those of the twentieth century. Another study that is of equal interest is the various faiths represented in hymnals. It is often surprising to learn that one's hymnal is a composite of hymns composed by people of other faiths than one's own. Another study might be made of hymns by American authors or English authors. Hunting for original words of a text that has been translated from another language, listing composers of a given century, studying hymn tune names—all of these and many other approaches make hymn study absorbing.

Every bit of service music for which the choir is responsible or in which it participates should be rehearsed weekly. Sunday-after-Sunday repetition of these too often makes them dull, matter of fact, and therefore meaningless unless they are freshly polished before each singing. If a processional and recessional are a part of the Sunday service, they need practicing from time to time lest the choristers become careless in their deportment.

In the development of a musician time must be allowed for him to listen to music as well as make it, for musical awareness and growth do not depend entirely upon the study of only such music as can be produced by a given group. Listening plays an important role in any aspect of education, and choristers who listen to music beyond their singing ability at the present are stimulated and challenged by it. They also learn to respect it.

Hearing live performances is ideal, but there are limits to what is presented in any given community. The next best possibility is to listen to recordings. There is much fine church music on records that the average listener will never have a chance to hear in any other way.

Selections for youth choirs must be made with care, keeping in mind the listeners' previous musical training. To expose teen-agers to the Bach B Minor Mass when all they have heard has been gospel tunes (heaven forbid!) would be defeating one's design. Listening periods are to be used purposefully—not as a time for daydreaming.

Anthems, hymns, oratorios, solos, and instrumental music suitable for church may be found in good recordings. If an oratorio is to be presented in one's own church or elsewhere in town, a recording of it can be listened to profitably in anticipation of hearing it live. If scores are available to follow during the listening, so much the better. This same practice may be followed with anthems to be sung by the adult choir on the following Sunday. In this case, the director should play the anthem on the piano while the choir listens with scores in hand. This would be monotonous if done routinely, but is valuable when there is something of special interest in the score.

Listening to recordings of hymns sung by outstanding choral groups is inspirational. It sometimes comes as a surprise to learn how beautiful hymns can be!

Quite aside from the gained familiarity with church music and the consequent quickening of interest in it, there are practical values for the singer as well. While listening to good recorded vocal music the chorister becomes increasingly aware of proper diction, phrasing, nuance in tone and color, and vocal line.

Vocal Techniques for Children and Youth by William C. Rice and myself includes extensive lists of recorded music in a variety of categories.

Recording one's own singing on tape helps in the learning process. This may be done in rehearsal, in which case it acts as a silent teacher, or in a service, after which it is valuable in analysis.

Taping of an individual's singing will help him to recognize his own deficiencies in pronunciation or pitch. This means of proving to him what he does is more effective than many words of the director. The same is true of group singing of course, for the tape will show up all elements of singing—tone, dynamics, diction, poor breathing, and phrasing and rhythmic faults.

A choir's evaluation of its public presentation as

recorded on tape is of inestimable worth for its future efforts. Hearing is believing!

Rehearsals should always end on a pleasant note. It is generally better to end by singing something that is nearly ready for presentation so that a feeling of accomplishment prevails. To close a rehearsal with a "problem" number will leave the singers feeling frustrated.

And finally—a few important reminders to the director:

1. Work fast.
2. Afford much variety.
3. Command—not demand—attention.
4. Keep a sense of humor.
5. Do a minimum of talking.
6. Encourage.
7. Show appreciation of work well done.
8. Require good posture.
9. Be alert.
10. Be friendly, but firm.
11. Be cheerful.

5

Using the Choirs

Since youth is naturally a time of restlessness, all organizations to which young people belong need to provide opportunities for action. A choir that sings only occasionally in Sunday service may feel a lack of sustained interest in the whole program. On the other hand, if there is a multiple choir program, it is obvious that every choir cannot sing alone each Sunday. Because we want them to feel that their responsibility is in leading in worship rather than performing an anthem, I believe that where it is at all possible each choir of junior age and above should be present in leadership capacity in the Sunday morning service. Chancel space may not be adequate for the seating of all choirs, but the front pews are rarely filled by the congregation, and choirs seated there have close proximity to the choir in the chancel and the minister. Choirs and minister, having made careful preparation for a service and working together in it, can animate the service to a surprising degree. Choirs so prepared become more at ease with the ritual of the service and develop a greater degree of interest in taking part. Weekly participation also helps them to realize and demonstrate that their individual anthem is a unit in the service rather than something to exploit them.

In churches where there is more than one Sunday morning service it will be impossible, and indeed inadvisable, for all choirs to be in each service. Responsibilities must be divided. It is to be hoped that the youth choir will not be made responsible every week for the less significant service. It happens sometimes that an early service is not well attended, and because the youth choir is available, it is asked to serve as the choir for that service. This is not giving youth an opportunity to see worship at its best and can bring disastrous results to a choir. The same thing can happen when the young people are solely responsible for a Sunday evening service. This service often uses music that is less than the best, and this poses a particular danger to youth. Don't let them get into the groove of leading a mediocre service!

Quite aside from all these considerations, it is seldom wise for a youth choir to present an anthem each Sunday. Because of vocal difficulties, and slowness in reading music on the part of some, it is often difficult if not impossible to prepare adequately an anthem a week. If it cannot be well presented, more harm than good comes from the attempt, and choristers can easily become satisfied with second- or even third-rate presentations. Anthems should not be repeated in less than a year's time unless there is some particular reason for doing so. Oft-repeated anthems are dulling to both singers and listeners. Let us never forget that anthems are for the purpose of contributing to the worship experience of all those present.

Singing with other choirs is stimulating and helpful. Many young choirs that sound fine in rehearsal suddenly grow timid when singing alone in the service. This is certain to be true with a group that is newly formed and has had no background of previous choir experience. Youth choirs often feel it beneath them to sing with any group in a lower age bracket but enjoy combining with adults from time to time, and there is much material available for such a procedure. Canons are popular—choirs singing antiphonally, with men and boys uniting on their parts and women and girls combining on theirs. Unison anthems make first-rate vehicles for matching diction and blending tone quality. These anthems often include a descant, and a group of high school girls with well-matched voices sound better on them than the soprano voices of older women. Other anthems provide for antiphonal singing between choirs or voice parts. A clever director can devise antiphonal material from conventional anthems and hymns.

There is not a wide selection of cantatas, and no big oratorios, for youth choirs, although the number of cantatas is growing. These choirs can successfully combine with adults in both areas, however. Some of the choruses can be sung alone, some of the solos can be sung by a group of teen-agers, or they may combine with adults only in certain portions.

Music drama has a special appeal for youth. Here again, there is not a great quantity of available material, but youth are creative enough to make their own. An episode, a theme may be agreed upon, appropriate dialogue and dramatic action added, and all this joined with suitable music. This music may be composed by one or more members of the choir, or it may be music they already know. Some very significant dramatic compositions have come from youth choir creators.

Such things as "The Feast of the Star," an Epiphany pageant by Bristol and Friedell in which there is physical action and spoken words as well as singing, can serve as models for creativity.

USING THE CHOIRS

Very excellent musical programs can be presented by youth choirs. These may be given on a Sunday afternoon or evening or for special groups within or without the church. If you, the director, let it be known that your choir is available for singing at men's clubs, women's auxiliaries, and other local functions, you will probably get more invitations than it is wise to accept. Unless you suggest the availability of the choir, however, such invitations may not be thought of, for people so often overlook the fact that choirs belong in the whole life of the church, not in Sunday services only. Singing in smaller meetings within the church will be of help to the choir in freeing them of self-consciousness and timidity.

Christmas is always a widely celebrated festival throughout the church, and because we have come to feel that singing is a necessary part of the celebration, choirs are in great demand. All choirs may combine in a carol sing or an anthem-hymn-carol service, and individual choirs may present cantatas or programs. There is much available material here for high school groups, possibly because school programs demand it. Caroling is popular at this season, and the youth choir can make its contribution to the church and community by preparing better than average singing groups for this activity. These choirs should extend their services throughout the year to hospitals, homes for the aged, and senior citizens' centers.

Exchange programs or combined programs with other churches animate and therefore benefit choristers. It often happens that more than one church is in a neighborhood, and their youth choirs enjoy singing in each other's churches or uniting and singing for each in turn.

Area or city-wide festivals are a high spot in the annual program of choirs throughout the country. In one city where several hundred young people participated in such a festival a parent was heard to say, "Isn't it wonderful what the churches are doing for our boys and girls? It is so good to see them here in such large numbers and to hear their beautiful singing. Now instead of wondering what to do on Sunday afternoon they look forward to their choir rehearsal."

Youth choirs can be valuable in helping to create interest in hymns and hymn singing. They may sponsor and lead hymn sings in their Sunday evening fellowship group, or may institute a season of hymn study for these meetings. The choir director can help, but youth leaders should carry most of the responsibility. The choir can present new hymns, rejuvenate well-known hymns, encourage the singing of some of them as canons, demonstrate how they can be used as anthems, and sing anthems based on hymn tunes. All this material can be used by them elsewhere and so serve a dual purpose.

The youth choir may sponsor a hymn festival for the whole church, asking other choirs to join them if desirable. They will enjoy selecting a theme for the festival and planning music around that theme.

Besides singing, young people are often capable of making other contributions to the music of the church, for many of them play band or orchestral instruments, piano, and sometimes organ. Combinations of these can well be used in hymn sings and festivals. Brass ensembles furnish lively and solid foundation for hymns and anthems, and they may be used for preludial music on festive days. Beautiful music is available for strings alone or for a combination of strings and woodwinds. Anthems with such accompaniment are especially lovely. Recorders are in high favor, and their flutelike quality is peculiarly suitable for descants. They may also be used as accompanying instruments.

Handbells have reached a high peak of popularity. Handbell choirs may accompany hymns and provide music for prelude or offertory. Some directors have the misguided idea that handbells are the solution to the problem of the changing voice—that is, they substitute bell ringing for singing. I am convinced, however, that boys who stop singing even for a little while seldom return to it. None of these instrumental activities should be put in place of singing but should enlarge the choristers' musical interests in the church.

Youth choirs make good musical missionaries. They can be of great help in interesting churches in good music, and they can stimulate another church to develop a comparable music program. Rural churches and small village churches that cannot have multiple choirs will welcome a program by a city youth choir. This program may be sung entirely by the young people, or they may invite the congregation to join them in singing hymns, using them as anthems, with descants, or as canons. This can breathe new life into hymn singing for the church.

Unless it is absolutely impossible, the singers should always be vested when singing as a choir unit. Vested choirs have eye appeal, but only if each chorister matches the others. Strict uniformity in the way a garment is worn is as important as having identical garments. Since young people are often careless in dress, they must be made aware that neatness and uniformity are required. They will not only look better and feel better, but they will actually sing better. Robes should be closed all the way to the hem so that pink, green, or yellow dresses are not seen. No blouse or sweater should show at the neckline. If the boys' shirt collars show, they must wear white shirts and uniform neckties. No jewelry, no hair ornaments, no bizarre hair arrangements must be seen. Choir hats or caps are one of uniformity's greatest aids, for distinguishing hair arrangements can attract immediate attention to individuals. There are numbers of styles of head covering, and most of them are becoming to young ladies. They must be worn at the same angle, however, and not tilted too far forward, backward, or to the side. Dignity must always be maintained. Girls should wear comfortable, low-heeled shoes because they cannot maintain good posture when tilted forward on very high heels. If a processional and recessional are a part of the service, it is doubly necessary that they wear comfortable walking shoes, uniform in color, preferably black. Haven't you seen choir women who, in processional, teetered on high heels, making it well nigh impossible for their partners to match their steps?

Vestments may be two-pieced or a single garment. In the initial purchase of them several things should be considered:

1. Shall the vestments of all the choirs be the same color and style? There is an advantage in having them identical except for size, thus making it possible to use them interchangeably between choirs as needed. Also, on those occasions when all choirs are combined, the uniform color and style are pleasing to the audience.

2. If color is used, what shall it be? When vestments are to be worn the year round, colors that look hot in summer should be avoided. Red, for example, is pretty in winter but makes the wearer look warm and the observer feel warm in summer. Ideally, a church will provide summer vestments of a lighter weight and color than are used in winter, but this is not always possible. Color selec-

tion must take into consideration the predominating colors used in the church, so as not to clash harshly with them or make them look dull or faded. Colors should "wear well" with the viewers—being something they feel comfortable with week after week. If each choir is vested in a distinctive color, it is necessary that each choir color blend with the others so as not to offend the eye when massed.

3. What style shall vestments be? Many things must be considered. What style will look equally well on everyone, yet be easily cared for, requiring the minimum expense in upkeep? A one-piece garment is less demanding of care, especially if the material is wrinkleproof. Where the two-piece cassock and cotta style is used, it is generally found that cottas need frequent pressing and laundering in order to look neat. One-piece garments need no decoration other than collars, but if desired, stoles of various kinds are available, and they add brightness to dark colors.

4. What material shall be used? Wrinkleproof material saves pressing time and presents a trimmer choir. It should not be too heavy to cause discomfort to the wearer but should have enough substance so as not to appear limp and lifeless. Washable materials are best for collars, of course, but vestments themselves look best when dry cleaned.

It is surely unnecessary to say that each vestment should be carefully fitted to its wearer, and that once fitted there be no change throughout the season unless the wearer grows in height. The habit of some choirs of dashing into their vestry and throwing on any available garment is deplorable. Vestments should be the right length and shoulder line for each wearer, and choir caps must be carefully fitted. After this, each wearer, with the help of choir mothers, is responsible for his vestment and his appearance.

Singing is the special prerogative of the youth choirs, but they also make good speaking choirs. Because they have experience in reading in their rehearsals, they can learn to do so with authority. They may effectively read the scripture in a service, or they may read antiphonally with the minister or other choirs. More suggestions for this activity are found in Chapter Eight.

We have spoken only of the group offerings of the choristers. Individual members of youth choirs are often good help with the music in church school classes, especially where the teacher is lacking in music training and ability. They make excellent helpers in the music for the vacation church school, and they can be fine assistants to the director of younger choirs. Some of them can play the piano as choir accompanists or in the church school, and some may be budding organists. They can assist with group singing at family night suppers and other weekday gatherings. All this will be valuable experience for the young people and worthwhile assistance to the music program of the church.

6

The Junior High Choir

Although school organization varies, the average
junior high school is made up of youth in grades
seven through nine, who are approximately twelve
to fourteen years of age. These are particularly
trying years for most young people, who are often
regarded by adults as "problems." People frequently
say of them that they are lazy, unresponsive, careless, and quite irresponsible, and while these descriptions may fit each of them at times, it cannot be
said that all of them are this way all the time. There
are vast individual differences even though they

seem to be so like each other. In order to work with them satisfactorily, the choir director must learn to know them individually as well as collectively. This will be a bit difficult, since he will see them most often in a group, but even here observation will tell him many things about them. Are they on friendly terms with each other—overgrown or underweight—shy or overbold—sulky or happy—careless in dress? Individual differences are not all on the surface and easily seen. Emotional and intellectual growth are individual matters too, with their variable patterns. Home environment is a factor to be recognized, as it is with every age. Sympathetic understanding of choristers' backgrounds will shed light on their attitudes and help the director in knowing how to deal with them.

The adolescent is beginning to see life in a new perspective, and his attitude toward it and his companions is changing rapidly. He is forming new friendships, developing new skills, and discovering new interests. Childhood, with its individualism, is being left behind, and a new gregariousness is emerging, for now boys and girls want to feel the security of a group. Perhaps they are overwhelmed by the complexities of a new adult life and need to feel that they are not alone in this venture. Whatever the reasons, this is a time when they join clubs and organized activity groups. This is a time when a choir at the church has a special appeal, but it will hold them only if it is made so interesting that its demands of time and energy are worthwhile. Restlessness is a normal, natural trait of the adolescent, and rather than being disturbed by it the wise director will put it to good use. Because these young people are constantly vacillating, much variety must be employed for them. Variety in music sung and listened to, variety in musical activities, variety in creative and intellectual approaches to music, are vitally necessary to youth.

Not all boys and girls of junior high age will be at the same stage of adolescence at the same time, but there are certain characteristics that are common to all of them. At twelve and thirteen years most girls are taller than boys and are usually more mature. They are more interested in boys than the boys are in them, and they try exaggerated means of being coquettish. Boys may enjoy this attempt to gain their attention, but they show annoyance and often become clownish and tend toward roughhousing. Because of rapid physical growth of bones and muscles both sexes are somewhat awkward and clumsy. Insecurity makes them self-conscious and gives them a feeling of inferiority. Clinging together in a group causes them frequently to take on an identical mood—commendable or troublesome. In the bibliography I have suggested helpful books to be read by workers with adolescents.

The adolescent feels an urgent need to be on his own, removed from parental control; yet there are times, many of them, when he yearns for adult guidance and supervision. Both sexes are full of enthusiasm, surprising energy, and an awakening interest in things aesthetic, though these qualities are not always on the surface. Increased emotional sensitivity makes them more responsive to beauty, and it is frequently true that their interest in religion is aroused by the attraction church arts have for them. Music, the most obviously emotional of the arts, speaks to them quickly and directly.

During the days of adolescence the voices of boys and girls undergo a maturing process, and this change takes place in accordance with their physical development. Since this is an individual matter, there will be several stages of voice development in any group of teen-agers. The problem of finding fitting materials for such a group is not an easy one.

The vocal cords of both sexes are lengthening and thickening, but those of boys are developing at a much more rapid pace than those of the girls. Boys also show a marked increase in the size of the larynx—in fact, this is one of the visible signs that voice change is beginning. All this alters the quality of voices, and it also produces a lowering pitch. Their vocal cords grow rapidly, but because supporting muscular growth is slower, it becomes impossible for boys to control their voices. Embarrassing sounds may come forth when they start to speak or sing. Sometimes, at this stage, boys become so self-conscious that they stop singing altogether,

71

or they try so hard to sing in a lower range before the voice is ready for it that they develop an unpleasant chesty tone. In former years it was thought that because of their vocal problems they should stop singing at this time, returning to it later when the voice was set. This resulted, as might be expected, in far too many abstinences from ever singing again. Today it is felt by most teachers of singing and choral directors that boys should sing through this period, but with vigilant guidance. Church choir directors may well follow the example of the public schools in this matter.

Because boys' voices create more problems for them and the choir director, girls' voices are sometimes neglected. The growth of their vocal cords is causing singing and speaking changes for them, too, but they are not as evident or as drastic as the changes in boys' voices. It will be well for us to consider boys and girls singly, but before we do that, let us look at some of the areas in which they will be mutually involved.

1. Part singing. The local public school music program and previous choir training will be determining factors in realizing the ability of these choristers to sing in parts. Though they must continue to sing in unison, most of their materials will be in two or more parts.

2. Diction. In order to sing well it is necessary to pronounce well. Young people frequently develop a bad habit of speaking carelessly and indistinctly.

3. Ear training. As long as music is studied, this subject must be pursued. Adding harmonies to melodies and singing in a new octave require attention now. Blending will also take on new proportions.

4. Music reading. Reading in the bass clef will be new for boys, and reading independent lines will probably be new for all.

5. Posture. Growing bodies use energy, and as a result young people often grow careless of posture and incline to droop and slump. Poor posture will produce faulty intonation and poor breathing, and diction will be neglected. The same rules for good posture must apply when sitting and standing.

6. Breathing. Right breathing habits must be promoted, for without them there can be no proper support of tone.

7. Blending. It is one thing to sing one's own part correctly but quite another to blend with other parts. It is necessary to learn to hear one's part in relation to another and to realize the harmonic structure of the whole.

JUNIOR HIGH GIRLS

It will be no surprise to find that girls concentrate better and learn faster when boys are absent! It is also true that their progress in part singing will be more rapid when they are not restrained by the vocal limitations of the boys. Alone, they can cover a far greater amount of material. Girls' voices, because of their similarity, make a pleasing singing ensemble in unison or in parts.

A separation of girls from boys abets the director also, for now he has more time to work closely with individual voices as their needs arise. Because boys' voices require so much attention, it is easy to slight the girls when they are together.

The range of junior high girls' voices is fairly uniform. Most of them are high and light, though some are adding new notes to their lower range and dropping a few from the top. It is most unusual to find a girl of this age with a real alto voice. Some voices will have a tendency toward breathiness and a certain husky quality. Physical appearance and the speaking voice will be some guide in judging the kind of voice a girl has.

Girls in their early teens may be expected to have a range of

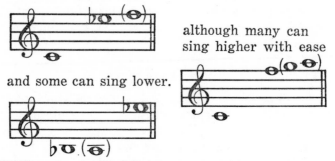

although many can sing higher with ease

and some can sing lower.

Their voices will fall into two general categories: first soprano and second soprano. Since the quality of these voices is so similar, their singing will show more blend of harmony than of color. Because their voices are so matched, they can sing equally well on each part, and they may advantageously change parts in various songs. This gives them the opportunity to learn to sing harmony parts as well as the melody, which is usually in the first soprano. This experience will be especially valuable to those who have not previously done part singing. Girls who read music well are too often required to sing a part that is too high or too low for them. This can do serious damage to the voice if kept up for a long time. The strain of constant singing in an uncomfortable range can damage vocal cords beyond later repair. It must also be remembered that girls in the early teens do not have much volume, and they must not be encouraged or allowed to try to force it. Dynamic changes in the music can best be made by reducing or adding the number of voices participating at a given time.

Each voice must be tested at the beginning of the choir year even though a girl has been promoted from a younger choir and the director is familiar with the voice. Many things can happen during a summer vacation. Testing should be repeated at a midway point in the choir season. Whether or not these tests should be given during a rehearsal or privately will be determined by the rapport between director and choristers and between the choristers themselves. If a fine feeling of friendliness exists, the choristers will benefit from hearing the testing. Tests should be brief and simple, consisting of singing up and down the first five notes of scales, starting each time a half step higher than previously. Scales and arpeggios are used in testing also.

Test for:

Range.

Pitch accuracy—is it different when singing high or low?

Tone quality—is it clear, reedy, breathy?

Volume—is it different high and/or low?

One of the first indications of voice change is when the singer finds high pitches more difficult to produce. Be wary, however, when a girl tells you she cannot reach a given pitch, for many of them feel they cannot reach one that is still in their voice range. When testing, do not let the singer see the piano keyboard!

Voice change is more obvious in some girls than others. I have observed many girls who never showed any marked variances in the voice during adolescence. The voices simply became gradually richer and fuller.

Song materials will include unison anthems, two- and three-part anthems, canons, descants, and hymns. These girls combine well with high school girls and adult women. They may also sing solo or duet sections in the anthems of the adult choir. The light quality of their voices is especially suited to descants, though care must be taken in selecting those in which the tessitura is not too high.

JUNIOR HIGH BOYS

Although girls' voices do not change greatly in quality, simply adding volume, fullness, and some change in range, boys develop entirely new voices. We can anticipate that most boys of junior high age will have changing voices, but that none of them will have completed the process. This may take from several months to several years. The larynx grows to twice its original size, and while this growth is taking place, voice control is arduous. The boy's speaking voice will first indicate that the change is starting, for it begins to lower and get husky. Some voices drop low very quickly while others lower gradually. Those voices that drop very low will tend to become higher later. Boys' speaking voices are a clearer indication of what they can sing than those of girls.

It is possible that there will be some boy sopranos in this group.

Their range will be about

and the tone quality will be more brilliant than that
of the girl soprano. The tone is light, with very little
volume but tremendous carrying power. Just before
the voice change these sopranos develop a very high
range, particularly if the voice has been previously
trained, and they often have a range of

Boys whose voices are still unchanged but who do
not have soprano quality have a range of about

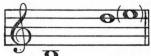   This voice is not as clear
as the soprano, and its quality is a little richer.

The range of the changing voice is quite varied,
of course, and sometimes it is limited to only five
or six notes.

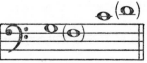

Again, the range may extend as much as an octave
or more.

Any of these ranges will be steadily changing, and the tone quality may be reedy, almost nasal at times, or it may be fairly rich. Boys can often sing for a longer period in the upper ranges of their voices than they think they can. In their desire to sing like men they are prone to cease trying to use their high voices. Like girls, they sometimes deceive themselves into believing that tones are too high.

When a voice narrows to a short range, boys become easily discouraged. They must be made to feel that this is a natural state of affairs and that they are not expected to sing anything that is not in their current range.

Boys' voices must be tested more frequently than girls' but may be given the same kind of tests. Watch their facial expressions for signs of tension and strain, especially on high tones. Strained, tense throats hurt. Downward vocalization is best and easiest. Listen to make certain the singer is not going into his chest voice as he descends.

Boys with changing voices commonly have difficulty in trying to match pitches in the lower register. As one boy said, "I can hear the pitch, Mrs. Ingram, but I simply can't find it!" Sometimes the inability to match these new pitches can be attributed to tension or anxiety. A relaxed atmosphere, plenty of time to hear the pitch, and sympathetic understanding are all needed.

What name shall we give this changing voice? The choice is yours. Irvin Cooper has made the name *cambiata* (from the Italian, meaning "changing") popular. He has arranged many songs for use by unchanged, changing, and changed (in early stages) voices. Another popular name for the changing voice is alto-tenor. Since the voices are neither alto nor tenor in quality, William C. Rice and I in *Vocal Technique for Children and Youth* have suggested that adolescent voices be classified as high, low, changing, and baritone.

Boys will need instruction in reading in a new clef, and until they learn to read reasonably well some time must be spent in this practice in each rehearsal. This should be made an interesting experience.

The director often finds it necessary to do his own arranging of song material for this group because of the uncertainty of numbers of changing voices and the state of their changing. When the vocal range is short, the boys can sing chord roots on a neutral syllable, or they can hum them. Songs that are harmonized by only a few chords are easiest for first experiences, others being added as skill develops. Chords, I, IV, V_7 are good starters. "The Lord Is My Shepherd," arranged by Lloyd Pfautsch, "Now Let Us All Praise God and Sing," by Gordon Young, and "My Shepherd Will Supply My Need," arranged by Marie Pooler are examples of anthems that may easily be adjusted to accomodate the short-range voice on chord roots.

80

Unison singing must not be abandoned, but careful consideration of range is required. Even then, some changing voices will doubtless find it necessary to drop out at either the high or the low extreme.

Boys enjoy singing with the men of the adult choir, and an all male choir makes a pleasant innovation in church services.

THE MIXED CHOIR

A mixed choir of adolescent boys and girls presents a variety of vocal problems, but the results of their work together can be highly satisfactory. A strong factor in favor of the mixed choir is that all other youth activities in the church are engaged in together, so it would seem quite natural to sing together in a choir. Also, larger numbers give greater strength in volume of singing, thus pleasing both singer and listener.

In a mixed choir of junior high age there will be a diversity of voices because of individual maturation. Total quality of the whole will be affected by the constantly changing range and quality of the boys' voices. There can be no satisfactory permanent balance of tone in this choir. There may be both boy and girl sopranos whose range is the same but whose quality differs. Any soprano solo parts in anthems should best be sung by one sex alone. As was suggested in the section about the boys' choir, the director will find it expedient to arrange the music for this group according to its abilities. Unison songs must have an easy range for both:

Boys with changing voices should never sing a unison melody an octave lower than the girls. The voice will be forced to reach lower than it can sing.

There will almost certainly be sight-reading difficulties with this group. The boys may learn to sing first by rote, then by position, but they must be encouraged to learn to read quickly and accurately. Girls can be helpful in the learning process by singing in unison with the boys—in their own octave, of course. Too much of this is bad for the morale of the boys, however. While the learning process of reading in the bass clef is still new, music that has slow-moving lower parts should be provided. The boys are learning to read in a new clef and manipulate a new voice at the same time.

Seating this choir may prove to be a bit difficult. Boy sopranos should sit near girl sopranos and at the same time sit in the male section. The same will be true of the altos. This is more easily accomplished if the church does not have a divided chancel, of course.

Song material should include unison anthems (some with descants for boy or girl sopranos), anthems for SAB, perhaps some SATB anthems if the male range is right, hymns, and canons. This choir may frequently join forces with the high school choir.

MUSIC MATERIALS

Whether we direct a combined choir of boys and girls or a separate choir for each, we need to keep the following things in mind as we select song materials for them:

1. The average range of the singers. This will remain fairly similar from year to year.

2. The tessitura. The average position of the notes—that is, where most of the singing will be done—is of more importance than the range. No music with a high or low tessitura should be used because no young voice can stand such a strain.

3. The limitations in dynamic ability. These voices are not strong and should not be forced to make big increases in volume.

4. The lack of agility. Girls' voices will have more agility than boys', but it is a thing that must be cultivated by both.

5. Reading ability. Here again, girls have the advantage, but the boys also should be reading increasingly involved parts.

6. The texts. By the time they reach junior high, boys and girls have been exposed to a great deal of prose and poetry, and it is to be hoped—and expected—that they have developed the ability to

discriminate between the inferior and the good. It is our duty to help them still further by seeing to it that texts we give them have literary merit and are representative of many centuries and cultures.

7. The music. Again, we must offer the best, for they will hear plenty of the other kind every day. Variety in rhythms, harmonies, and melodies must be provided, and these too should be typical of various periods and civilizations. Neither text nor tune should subscribe to temporary faddism.

8. The use to which the material will be put. Most, if not all, of the music learned will be sung in church services and gatherings. Selection must be made on the basis of its suitability for this usage.

9. The accompaniment. Although *a cappella* singing will be practiced in rehearsal, an instrumental accompaniment will give the singers more security in public. Make certain that the accompaniment is not so full and elaborate as to cover their voices, nor so difficult that the accompanist cannot play it well.

10. The cost. The church with an unlimited, or even adequate, music budget is rare; therefore, a sensible selection of music for long-range use is necessary. Anthem collections are cheaper than individual numbers bought separately, but unless more than half the numbers are usable by one's specific group, they are no bargain. Of course such

collections must be augmented by anthems in octavo form, and several should be added to the choir library each year, always keeping in mind their usefulness with future choirs as well as the present one. Memorization of music should be continued, and this is practical when choirs are combining, thus using one set of anthems for rehearsals rather than purchasing many copies.

7

The Senior High Choir

This choir is made up of boys and girls in senior high school, grades ten through twelve, whose ages are approximately fifteen to eighteen. This choir can do many of the things an adult choir can do, and often can do them better! The biggest differences lie in volume, quality, and range of voice. This choir should be treated more like adults than children, though they are still struggling in the direction of maturity. They still possess many childish traits and much emotional instability, but are mentally capable of adult understanding. Artistic interpretation of both the sung and the spoken word is now more fully possible.

Prior to this age girls have usually been ahead of boys in physical development, but by the time senior high is reached this growth becomes more uniform. Both sexes are beginning to show more poise and less awkwardness. They are becoming less selfish and tend to show a real concern and affection for others, even those outside their immediate group. Romances between the sexes spring up, but because of the general emotional instability of this age, they are often of short duration. Firm friendships are developed between members of the same sex.

These young people have as marked a tendency to move in gangs as is found among the junior high age. That they have not become independent individuals is evidenced by the way they all wear the same kind of clothes, jewelry, and hair styles. Because they enjoy clubs and social groups, especially those that include the opposite sex, a choir can appeal to them. As with the junior highs, the choir must be worth their time and energy. Discipline of such a choir must be firm, for young people both expect and respect it. The director must do all in his power to discourage cliques within the choir, for this is not a group designed for social purposes, but a group to lead in church worship, and it must function as a unit.

A choir made up of members who have had

previous choir training is ideal, for a good choir does not develop overnight, but only after careful work has been done over a period of time. However, new people are constantly coming to a church, and their families may want to join one of the choirs. What shall we do with young people who apply for membership but who have limited or even no previous choir experience? First of all, we must remember that though we want a choir that sounds well, the church is seeking to provide musical experience for all its members. Our aim is to combine music and worship in a meaningful way so that they stimulate the spirit of youth. Can we then deny choir membership to any who apply? This is a matter for the individual director to decide in the light of his situation and convictions.

When accepting a new member who has not previously been in a choir, the director should determine if he can carry a tune, has a good ear, can read music, and has a blending voice. Certainly those less qualified applicants will require individual help of the director, and such time may not be available. Or, if the choir functions weekly in services, the learning and polishing process will have to be done quickly, and several droners will be a big handicap. If they are admitted, they may be seated beside strong leaders who are willing to be helpful. These leaders must be secure enough not to be distracted by wrong pitches, and they must have a sincere desire to help. Inexperienced singers whose ears are good learn quickly from those who are skilled. They will need to feel successful as often as possible, and if there are many inexperienced ones in a choir, some of the music must be geared to them. It must be remembered that this is not a school choir of selected voices and balanced parts.

With boys and girls both in this choir we must use music that is entirely suitable for their vocal aptitudes. The voices of neither sex are completely through the changing process, though there is more steadiness in both and many things previously sought can now come into fruition. High school people like to be challenged and their music must do this to them. If it is too easy, boredom and indifference will result.

Although voices in high school are still changing individually we can have reasonable expectations about the voices of the girls. Their voices will still be light, and there will not be a great deal of difference in the ranges of first and second soprano. A comfortable singing range for them, though some can go higher and some lower, is

We seldom find in this age a wobbly, tremulous voice such as we frequently find in mature sopranos.

Such voices cause a group to sound out of tune, since they do not remain firmly fixed on a given pitch and cannot blend well with other voices. They are usually caused by lack of training or poor training, but they can result when voices are taxed beyond their limit.

An alto voice is beginning to emerge, though it is still light, and it is rare to find a voice with real contralto quality. Their comfortable ranges are

1st alto   2nd alto

By now boys' voices have passed through the early stages of mutation and are becoming more settled. We can classify them as tenor and bass. Such classification cannot be final, however, for those who seem at first to be tenors may very well become baritones. High school tenors have voices that are still imperfect, especially in the upper range, since the development of this voice takes a longer time than the development of the bass voice. Voices that are likely eventually to be tenors have a tendency to lower more slowly than the basses. The tone quality of young tenor voices will vary, some tending toward the mature, adult quality while others still preserve the child voice characteristics.

Comfortable singing ranges for tenors are

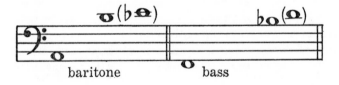

1st tenor   2nd tenor

All tenors should go into falsetto on notes that are too high for them. Properly used, falsetto is of much value in the development of their voices, especially in helping to make them flexible and extending their range.

A low bass voice is rare in high schools but is not unheard of. The majority of the lower voices are baritone, though they will probably have divergent ranges. This voice sounds more mature than the tenor and is surprisingly full at times.

baritone   bass

Always keep your ears open for the boys who want to sing high or low notes too soon. It may be easy to vocalize on them, but it is quite another thing to sing them. Boys' voices will probably show a remarkable change following a summer vacation, for many things can happen to them in two or three months. Frequent testing is required.

In choirs where only a three-part division is used

(SAB), the ranges are designated as approximately

soprano   alto   baritone

High schools choirs will be concentrating on the same vocal and interpretive elements that concerned the junior highs, but with a few additions.

1. Vocalization. Perhaps for the first time they will be interested in vocalization for its own sake. Whether the vocalization comes at the beginning of a rehearsal as a kind of warm-up or later in the rehearsal as a change of pace, it should never be done perfunctorily. This is a good time to work on blending, as well as agility and extension of range. Vocal exercises are most interesting when there is a connection between them and music that is being learned. The same vocalises sung week after week are of little value because the singers soon tire of them and become inattentive while they are being sung.

2. Flexibility. Now that the "new" voices are becoming more comfortable, more time should be spent in working for flexibility. Staccato and legato phrases and running passages are important in voice development and should be practiced on a variety of syllables that permit the singers' throats to be open—"oo," "ah," "oh." Girls' voices are more flexible than those of boys, and for obvious reasons.

3. Tuning. The differences in male and female voice qualities create a problem in tuning. In the earlier stages of learning to tune it is easier if one voice part sings first alone with the others listening, then continues to hold while each section enters alone and holds its note.

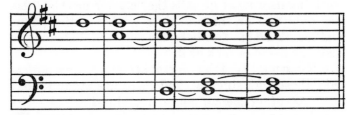

Another procedure is to have the bass and soprano sing in octaves, with the alto, then tenor, entering later.

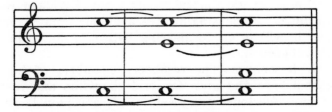

These and similar exercises should be practiced first on the syllable "ah" to get the feel of the open throat and relaxed jaw necessary to good singing. Other syllables may be used later, but they must not be those that tend to close the throat. These exercises may also be practiced on vowel sounds that are open. Such exercises may be hummed as well as sung, making certain to open the mouth slightly while so doing. When directing practice blending on syllables, vowels, consonants, or humming, Donald Kettring uses what he calls the "cluster method." He has only two or three singers work together, thus making it easier for both singers and listeners to hear the blend or lack of it.

4. Tone quality. If universal acclaim is any indication, those folk singers (and there are many kinds) with a rather nasal, plaintive, slurring tone are popular, and teen-agers tend to imitate them. We must keep before them the knowledge that the ideal voice is one that is free of tension, has no nasal quality (except when needed), and is produced when the throat is open. A closed throat is not flexible, and it produces pinched, reedy tones. Excellent recordings of fine singing are available, and young people will profit by hearing both solo voices and choral groups.

5. Resonance. The resonance chambers of high school boys and girls are still changing, and few, if any, overtones are produced. If a person learns to sing properly, his resonators work for him automatically. Again a free, open throat must be emphasized, for resonance will not be possible without it. Correct pronunciation also helps.

Of course reminders about good posture and proper breathing must be made, and continued work in improving music reading is necessary. Ear training should be continued in every rehearsal.

One of the things that the high school choir should do more frequently than the junior highs is to sing, or at least practice, *a cappella.* The choir will very likely be too unbalanced in parts to do a creditable job of singing *a cappella* publicly, but there is much to be gained by singing unaccompanied in practice sessions. Besides being excellent ear training and an energizing challenge to the singers, *a cappella* singing impresses upon them the need to listen, the importance of good tone, the need to phrase exactly, the necessity for blend and balance, and the importance of understanding the music harmonically as well as tonally.

Now and then a director, carried away with his enthusiasm for *a cappella* singing, overemphasizes it with his choir and denies them the friendship with accompanied music. Pure *a cappella* singing is the result of long, hard practice, and there is not enough time in most choir programs to perfect it. Its value lies in the sensitivity it develops in singers. Remember to begin the practice of it with numbers that are not difficult and that have rhythms and chord structure that are not intricate.

Song material for the high school choir will include unison anthems, anthems for SATB and SAB, hymns, canons, chorales, and cantatas. This group may satisfactorily join forces with the junior high choir or the adult choir. People of senior high age are sometimes included in the adult choir, as has been said before, though they usually prefer to be in a group of all teen-agers.

This choir makes an even better speech choir than the junior highs because they have more variety of tone color. Such groups can present beautiful choral effects entirely without music. There are 136 psalms that are clearly antiphonal and that may be read with excellent effect by high schoolers. The choristers benefit from "student-directing," the speaking group as well as the singing group, thus giving profit to themselves and help to the director, who is often the organist as well.

So far, nothing has been said about rhythmic interpretation for junior or senior highs. If this form of expression has been started with children at an early age, it is natural for them to want to continue it. If such has not been the case, it is more difficult for older youth to lose their self-consciousness. Teen-age girls will respond more quickly than boys, but both can be drawn into worship through movement. Such movement may be employed with the spoken word as well as with music. It will be necessary to appeal to the boys through manly interpretations rather than movements that are subtle and seemingly effeminate to them. A choir camp presents a fine atmosphere for introducing this sacred art form.

One service in which rhythmic interpretation combined particularly effectively with music and spoken word was one I directed in Memorial Methodist Church, Lynchburg, Virginia. All choirs and the minister participated in what we termed "The Christian Year in Music and Movement." The entire cycle of the seasons of the year was represented. The minister read appropriate scripture, the choirs sang anthems applying to the particular season, and the whole church sang fitting hymns. Each season was interpreted in movement by members from one or another of the seven choirs. High school girls helped to create the interpretations and train the younger children. Acolytes changed the paraments, and the minister changed his stole to show the proper color for each season. The whole service was highly instructional as well as enjoyable.

Rhythmic interpretation by junior and senior high choristers is often used in seasonal services such as those at Christmas and Easter, and in connection with cantatas sung by the adult choir. Older youth are especially creative in this area and find it comparable to singing in releasing emotions. In my experience it has been of enormous help in getting teen-agers over emotional hurdles.

As was stated in the previous chapter, young people have a flair for drama and enjoy creating as well as participating in it. In their creations they have a wonderful opportunity to correlate music with the spoken word and dramatic action.

Small groups from the choir may make up singing

ensembles that will be available for use at class meetings, men's clubs, and ladies' auxiliary meetings. There will undoubtedly be some soloists among this age group, and they may make their contribution to services and group gatherings.

The church *needs* high school choirs.

High school singers *need* the church.

8

The Speech Choir

Choric speaking has had a great revival in our country in the twentieth century, and speech choirs are being formed more and more frequently in our churches. This style of speaking is especially attractive to young people, and they are usually the ones who are components of such choirs.

Choric speaking is not new, for it has been used in some form or other since the days of early Greek drama. In most present-day churches people speak unitedly during certain prayers and responses, and they speak antiphonally with the minister in responsive readings. Because such speaking is not rehearsed, it is often treated in a dull, uninteresting, half-meant, half-understood manner.

Earlier in this century, verse speaking choirs became popular in England, and their popularity spread to the United States. We have extended the boundary of verse speaking to include speaking of prose as well, and we are making use of speech choirs in schools, colleges, and churches.

Besides being of interest to young people, such choirs are of great benefit to them at a time when their singing voices are not at their best. In order to speak well, the same techniques must be used as when singing well, and the same disciplines must be adhered to. As in singing, each member must carry his full share of responsibility, yet must submerge self to the whole. Individual vocal problems caused by voice change are not as evident in speaking as in singing; therefore, self-consciousness is minimized.

Speaking voices are usually grouped as for singing—high, medium, low. Again, the speaking voice will give some indication of pitch range, though since many people do not make full use of their pitch range, this will not be a complete indication of potential.

Vocal drills are necessary for good speaking. Such drills are comparable to those used in singing, the only difference being that the sounds are spoken rather than sung. Exercises involving staccato and legato, crescendo and diminuendo, accent, intensity, and facility of lips and tongue are essential.

Marjorie Gullan includes rhymes and poems to be used at first rehearsals of a speech choir in her book *The Speech Choir*. She also gives clear instructions as to proper reading of each. This book should be at hand for every director of a speaking group.

Elizabeth von Hesse has a chapter titled "The Velvet Tone" in her book *So to Speak*. She describes such tone as a necessary element of a pleasing voice that also has carrying power. While this book deals largely with the individual voice of a public speaker, this writer has adapted many of her suggestions to group speaking.

Conveying the message of words without music places new demands on the choristers. They must first understand the meaning of the text to be spoken. By understanding what words mean, we instinctively give them their individual tone color and thus are able to give them the mood their author intended. Great care must be taken to avoid artificial sounds. There must be variety in pitch, in volume, in speed, and there must be points—or a point—of emphasis. All these must be created by the speakers. The director must decide where solo voices would be appropriate, where intensity can be built up by the addition of other voices, where the main stress must be made, and how much volume to give the whole. They are practicing the making of melody as voices modulate in unison from one pitch to another, and the making of harmony as voices blend, each on his own pitch level. It is surely unnecessary to say that good speech can never result when posture is poor!

Two elements that are automatically prepared for the singer and not for the speaker are time and rhythm. By timing we mean the length of time allotted between words, phrases, or sentences. Proper timing adds to the dramatic effect of the whole or utterly destroys it. This calls for good judgment on the part of the speakers. Pauses for silence must not be too long or too short, but must give the listener proper time to assimilate what is being said. Pauses may be used after words or phrases to underline them. If they are made before, they help to induce suspense.

The rhythm in which a selection is spoken is not determined by pre-set signs as in music scores. Rather, it is suggested by the central idea of the text, plus the length of the sentences.

First the basic rhythm must be found; then ways of varying it satisfactorily must be decided. Care must be taken not to read in the singsong way of little children (and sometimes ministers!). If there is a central figure about whom the text revolves, a study of that figure will likely help to determine the rhythmic pace at which he moves, and hence the pace to be used when speaking about him. The gentleness of Francis of Assisi, the calmness of Job, the high tension of Job's wife, the vigor of

Noah—all these can be expressed by the way we speak of them. Rhythmic pace for scenic descriptions will be determined by whether or not the scene is of pastoral quiet or the bustle of a city.

Materials for use by speaking choirs in the church must be varied. They may include Bible readings, poetry, prose, and drama. Religious drama can be read effectively without dramatic action. Speech choirs may read the scripture at Sunday church services either alone or antiphonally with the minister. A well-prepared choir can add fresh meaning to any text. A speaking group may be used in musical services to provide the link between songs. A program in which the story of Christmas is presented chronologically is highly effective when a speech choir reads each of the sequences and a song about the same event follows. The reading should be varied, of course, making use of soloists and small ensembles, as well as the entire group.

A service based on psalms lends itself well to spoken and sung words. Responsorial parts may be read between choir, minister, and congregation, or any arrangement of these. Interesting treatment of the text is displayed through reading followed by a musical arrangement of the same psalm. If the psalm has been made metrical and a hymn tune set to it, the congregation will enjoy singing it with the choirs.

As suggested before, using a central figure as a topic presents a variety of means of expression.

When the rhythmic choir and the adult choir in my church presented the cantata "Job" by Roberta Bitgood, the speech choir first spoke the text. They followed the pattern used later by the singers—a single voice spoke the part of Job, another that of Satan, the Lord, Job's wife. This helped to prepare the congregation, as it reminded them of the text and the individuals who had leading parts in the Bible story.

During a vacation church school a junior high age class learned "The Canticle to the Sun." Here again there is opportunity for individual as well as group speaking. On the concluding day of the school a program was given in which they spoke this canticle. Then the younger children sang the hymn arranged from it, "All Creatures of Our God and King," and a group of juniors gave an interpretation in movement.

The speech choir provides excellent accompaniment for a rhythmic choir. The speaking may or may not be interspersed with instrumental or sung music. I have on numberless occasions used the speech choir speaking alone while the movement group remained passive in tableau. Then they moved to instrumental music as they interpreted what had been spoken. Thus, by first hearing and then seeing, the congregation had the advantage of double emphasis on the thought.

In most of our churches a speech choir will likely be a part of a singing choir. These choirs often develop when the singing voices are undergoing change and when the adolescent needs to be challenged with fresh interests. Speaking experiences are of the utmost value, as they tend to keep him before the public in performance capacity, as they improve all the elements he uses in singing, and as they help him to continue to learn self-discipline.

9

Music Resources

Many things must be kept in mind when considering materials for teen-age choirs. The amount of money that can be spent is of primary importance and carries with it the challenge of trying to get the most for that money. The size of the choirs and their musical abilities must be taken into account. All tendencies to be overambitious or overcautious for them must be curbed. Usefulness of the music for future choirs is an important factor for consideration. Since the music will be used in worship services, we must make certain that it is appropriate for use in our particular church and denomination.

What the music says—the text—is of such great importance we must make certain that it meets our requirements. Does it meander, dawdle, say the same thing over and over? Is it sentimental, vague, ambiguous? Does it channel our thoughts? Texts should convey a sagacious message, intelligently expressed, and theologically in accord with the tenets of our church. They should speak directly to twentieth-century people. They need not have been written in this century in order to speak to us, however, for the message found in many an old verse is so timely that it has lost nothing with age. Texts also serve as teaching material, for they influence youth in right ways of thinking and acting.

One more thing to consider while examining texts is the matter of relevance to the choir itself. Do they express intellectually and emotionally what young people may understand and feel? We expect the message presented by the choir to have authority, but this cannot come to pass unless the singers believe the words they sing.

Does the music remind us of popular musical shows—of TV commercials—of concert halls—of opera? There was a time when opera and popular instrumental music were arranged for church use by adding pseudo-religious words. Anthems and solos of this nature are a distraction to worship. Worship music need not be dull, slow, ponderous, and devoid of beautiful melody. It can be gay and still be worshipful. Folk tunes and contemporary music as well as plainsong, psalm tunes, and chorales can all be used as vehicles in worship.

If the music fits our requirements, we must then examine it to discover how it fits the text. Is the rhythm of the music suited to the mood of the words? Does the tune fit the words, or are there awkward divisions of syllables? Are the phrases too long to permit ease of breathing? Is the text pointed up by the music, or does the music interfere by taking a too prominent place?

The library must contain a variety of anthems. We will need anthems to fit the various patterns of worship—praise, prayer, commitment—and the seasons of the church year. Then there must be anthems of general nature, as well as some for festival times. There must be variety in the music as well as in the subject matter. Young people like contemporary music better than their elders do, and they learn it much more quickly. Care must be exercised in the selection of this music, however, because it should be music that will wear well beyond its initial presentation. Plainsong appeals to youth, and they sing it well. There are many folk tunes and early hymn tune arrangements that fit requirements of both text and tune.

Music that is contrapuntal is undesirable for a choir that is unable to hold its own in sections. All voices entering at the same time and moving together seems to give needed security. We do want

to watch out for music that has too much repetition
of harmony, however, for it can be very dull. Attractive rhythms will help to offset repetitious harmony.

Avoid watered-down arrangements of difficult anthems. If they cannot be sung in the original, it is
usually better to shun them. There is so much good
music available for youth that they need not reach
over into things they can do better later in life.

Another thing to avoid is simplified large works.
Many an arranger has so simplified the choruses
of great oratorios, passions, and masses that they
bear only a frail resemblance to the originals. Let's
stimulate young people to make the acquaintance
of these great works, but sing them only when their
voices are ready for them.

Remember that hymns make excellent anthem
material, and the hymnals are already at hand.
Lovelace and Rice in *Music and Worship in the
Church* suggest many ways of using hymns as
anthems, and you and your young people may think
of others.

Descants may be taught by rote so there is no
need for the library to have more than one copy.
Rounds and uninvolved canons may also be taught
by rote.

Because fellowship is of prime importance to
young people, they enjoy singing what may be
termed "fun" songs, and while it would be impracti-
cal to spend much valuable rehearsal time in such
relaxed, undisciplined singing, there may very well

be times when they fill a real purpose. Booklets, such as those published by the Cooperative Recreation Service, Delaware, Ohio, provide good materials at a low cost.

A good collection of records should belong to any church music library, though money for their purchase is not always available. A few well-chosen hints here and there might result in a fund for such a purpose. A really good record player is a necessity, of course, and a tape recorder is a valuable asset. Films and filmstrips are also desirable and useful. These may be rented rather than owned, though it is highly practical for a church to own its own filmstrips so that they are available for repeated use.

ANTHEM AND SONG BOOK COLLECTIONS

Curry: Anthems for the Youth Choir, Book 1 (Westminister).

Davis: The Green Hill Three-Part Sacred Music for Women's Voices (E. C. Schirmer 1838).

Drischner: Make a Joyful Noise (Concordia 97-4685).

Ehret, ed.: Sing Praises (Broadman 451-757).

Ehret, ed.: Sing Praises, II (Broadman 451-765).

Ehret: Sing We to God (C. Fischer 04263).

Lovelace: Collection for Soprano, Alto, Tenor (Canyon 6450-2).

Ringwald, ed.: Praise Him (Shawnee G-15).

Thomas: The Morning Star Choir Book (Concordia 97-6287).

Thomas: A Second Morning Star Choir Book (Concordia 97-4702).

MUSIC RESOURCES

Thomas: The SSA Chorale Book (Concordia 97-7592).

Wienhorst: Four 18th-Century English Rounds (Concordia 98-1668).

Willan: Carols for the Seasons (Concordia 97-6319).

Willan, ed.: Sing Praises, Vols. 1 and 2 (Concordia CC 1032, 97-7610).

Williams: Twelve Anthems for SAB (Summy-Birchard 2212).

SATB ANTHEMS

Bach: At Thy Feet (B. F. Wood 44-241).

Bach: A Child Is Born in Bethlehem (Concordia 98-1803).

Bach: Jesu, Joy of Man's Desiring (E. C. Schirmer 317).

Bach: Now Winter Fades from Sight (J. Fischer 7816).

Billings: When Jesus Wept (Mercury 102).

Bitgood: Hosanna (Gray 1345).

Butler: All Nature's Works His Praise Declare (Hope CH-627).

Buxtehude: God Shall Do My Advising (Concordia 98-1449).

Clokey: I Sing as I Arise Today (Concordia 98-2017).

Davis: Alleluia, Come, Good People (Galaxy 1132).

Davis: As It Fell Upon a Night (Galaxy 1291).

Diercks: Clap Your Hands (Abingdon APM-103).

Dietterich: Carol of the Advent (Abingdon APM-216).

Edmunds: Five Dutch Carols (Concordia 98-1775).

Ehret: Calvary's Mountain (Elkan-Vogel 1210).

Ehret: Walking Along to Bethlehem (Elkan-Vogel 1166).

Grams, arr.: On Christmas Night (Concordia 98-1760).

Gregory: Jesus, Our Lord Is Crucified (Hope A-324).

Holst: A Festival Chime (Galaxy 8).

Kitson: Jesu, Grant Me This, I Pray (Oxford A57).

Lapo: Lord of All Being (Row 445).

Larson: To God All Praise and Glory (Summy-Birchard B2095).

Lockwood, arr.: All Thy Works Praise Thee (Gray 1067).

Lotti: Joy Fills the Morning (Gray 172).

Lovelace: God Is My Strong Salvation (Canyon 5403).

Lovelace: I Sing th' Almighty Power of God (Canyon 5802).

Lovelace: O Thou Eternal Christ, Ride on! (Abingdon APM-105).

Lovelace: Talk With Us, Lord (Summy-Birchard 1545).

Lovelace: What Shall I Render to My God (Canyon 5503).

McAfee: Lord, Make Me an Instrument of Thy Peace (Walton 2061).

McAfee: Psalm Ninety-Two (Walton 2084).

Marshall: Awake My Heart and Render (Gray 2515).

Mendelssohn: The Lord Is a Mighty God (Kjos 9).

Niles: Jesus, Jesus, Rest Your Head (G. Shirmer 8302).

Peek: Now Glad of Heart Be Every One (Canyon 5303).

Pfautsch: Sing Praise to God (Summy-Birchard 5315).

Pooler: Be Thou My Vision (Augsburg 1155).

Reed: Rise Up, O Men of God (J. Fischer 8004).

Rowley: Praise (Oxford A24).

Sateren: Christ Is the World's True Light (Concordia 98-1800).

Sateren: In the Moon of Wintertime (Canyon 6213).

Shaw: With a Voice of Singing (Curwen 8103).

Thiman: Angels Holy, High, and Lowly (C. Fischer PT-1637).

MUSIC RESOURCES

Thiman: Immortal, Invisible (Novello 1140).

Thomson: My Shepherd Will Supply My Need (Gray 2046).

Wienhorst: Awake, My Soul, and All Praise to Thee (Concordia 98-1791).

Williams, D. H.: A Hymn for Thanksgiving (Summy-Birchard B-279).

Williams, V., arr.: The Old Hundredth Psalm Tune (Oxford).

Young, C.: All Nature's Works His Praise Declare (Canyon 6203).

Young, C.: Be Thou My Vision (Kjos 5254).

Young, C.: Day by Day, Dear Lord (Hope A-359).

Young, G.: Build Thee More Stately Mansions (Presser 312-40405).

SAB ANTHEMS

Bach: Awake, My Soul, and Sing Ye (Wood 44-548).

Billings-Copes: Shepherd's Carol (Gray 2667).

Caldwell, arr.: Tell Us, Shepherd Maids (Gray 2358).

Croft: O Give Thanks unto the Lord (Concordia 98-1788).

Davis, arr.: Good King Wenceslas (Summy-Birchard 1533).

Dietterich: Immortal Love, Forever Full (Abingdon APM-214).

Hill: The Whole Bright World Rejoices (Gray 1861).

Hokanson: Praise to the Lord (FitzSimons 6011).

König-Nelson: Oh, That I Had a Thousand Voices (Augsburg 1167).

Lenel: Come, Ye Faithful, Raise the Strain (Concordia 98-1384).

Leupold, arr.: Immortal, Invisible (Concordia 1440).

Licht: Ave Verm (Flammer 88637).

Lotti: Mighty Lord, Thy Faithfulness (E. C. Schirmer 1716).

Lotti: Surely He Hath Borne Our Griefs (E. C. Schirmer 1124).

Lovelace: Hymn of Nations (Canyon 5701).

Nelson: Hosanna to the Son of David (Augsburg 1258).

Shaw, G.: Praise God in His Holiness (G. Schirmer 8574).

Shaw, M.: Let All the People Praise Thee, O God (Novello 1267).

Thatcher: Come, Ye Faithful (Oxford E-11).

Willan: Sing to the Lord of Harvest (Concordia 98-1451).

UNISON AND UNISON WITH DESCANT

Darst: O God of Youth (Gray 2147).

Davies: May the Grace of Christ (Novello CS-73).

Davis: Let All Things Now Living (E. C. Schirmer 1819).

Frauenholtz: Jesus, Thanks to Thee We Offer (Concordia 98-1827).

Hammerschmidt: Let the People Praise Thee, O God (Concordia 98-1826).

Jacob: Brother James's Air (Oxford OSC1139).

Johnson: Carol of the Singing Reeds (J. Fischer 7710).

Lenel: All Praise to Thee, Eternal God (Concordia 98-1402).

Lindeman: Long Hast Thou Stood, O Church of God (E. C. Schirmer 1765).

Lovelace: The Darkness Now Has Taken Flight (Abingdon APM-302).

Marcello: Lord, Who Shall Dwell upon Thy Holy Hill? (Concordia 98-1551).

MUSIC RESOURCES

Marcello: O Lord God, Who Dwelleth with Thee? (Concordia 98-1550).

Marcello: O Lord, Our Governor (Concordia 98-1045).

Purvis: What Strangers Are These? (Summy-Birchard B-969).

Stanton: Christ Is the World's True Light (Oxford E36).

Thiman: Grant Us Light (G. Schirmer 10280).

Thiman: A Seasonal Thanksgiving (G. Schirmer 10738).

Van Iderstine: God Rest Ye Merry, Gentlemen (Abingdon APM-124).

SSA ANTHEMS

Coggin: He Was Despised (Hope A-352).

Davis: Mary's Lullaby (Summy-Birchard B-142).

Dickinson: O Nightingale, Awake (Gray 230).

Diemer: Alleluia (C. Fischer CM-7289).

Diemer: A Christmas Carol (C. Fischer CM-7262).

Ehret: Shepherds, Shake Off Your Drowsy Sleep (Mercury MC-268).

Hallstrom: Shepherds Awake (Shawnee B1114).

Lotti: Surely He Hath Borne Our Griefs (E. C. Schirmer 1509).

Luvaas: Alleluia, Christ Is Born (Summy-Birchard 1543).

Mackinnon: Give to My Restless Heart, O God (Gray 844).

Pergolesi: Glory to God in the Highest (Flammer 89041).

Pfautsch: Five Narrative Carols (Summy-Birchard B-1616).

Reger: The Virgin's Slumber Song (Associated Music Publishers A-91).

Willan: Glory to God in the Highest (Concordia 98-1428).

Willan: Sing to the Lord of Harvest (Concordia 98-1450).

SA ANTHEMS

Brook: The Shepherd (Oxford 149).

Cassler, arr.: While By My Sheep I Watch at Night (Augsburg 1437).

Davis: Jesus, Sleeping in the Manger (Summy-Birchard 4121).

Dvořák: I Will Sing Thee Songs of Gladness (G. Schirmer 8646).

Fauré: Jesu, Word of God Incarnate (E. C. Schirmer 860).

Fauré: Sanctus (FitzSimons 5017).

Franck: At the Cradle (E. C. Schirmer 1533).

Hallstrom: The Snow Lay on the Ground (Shawnee 5).

Hassler: Crucified Also for Us (E. C. Schirmer 1918).

Kountz: Rise Up Early (Galaxy 1701-8).

McAfee: In Heavenly Love Abiding (Canyon 6601).

Marcello: And With Songs I Will Celebrate (Concordia 98-1047).

Marcello: Give Ear unto Me (Gray 1522).

Pooler, arr.: A Child Is Born in Bethlehem (Augsburg TC15).

Pooler, arr.: Come, Thou Long Expected Jesus (Augsburg 1362).

Pooler: Hosanna Now Through Advent (Augsburg 1439).

Schalk: God of Mercy, God of Grace (Concordia 98-2007).

Schalk, arr.: Two-Part Canons (Concordia 98-1763).

Vigeland: My Faith, It Is an Oaken Staff (Gray 2698).

Warner: Let Us, With a Gladsome Mind (Summy Birchard 2063).

Warner: Sing We Noel (Gray 2723).

White: A Prayer of St. Richard of Chichester (Oxford E43).

MUSIC RESOURCES

Whittlesey: We Tread Upon Thy Carpets (Flammer 86153).

Wienhorst: Chorale Settings for the Seasons (Concordia 98-1129).

Willan: The King Ascendeth into Heaven (Concordia 98-1381).

Willan: Rejoice in the Lord Alway (Concordia 98-1815).

Williams: A Hymn for Thanksgiving (Summy-Birchard B-218).

Young: Bring a Torch, Jeanette (Hope A-370).

Bibliography

Anderson, Virgil. *Training the Speaking Voice.* New York: Oxford University Press, 1942.

Andrews, Frances M., and Leeder, Joseph A. *Guiding Junior High School Students in Music Experiences.* Englewood Cliffs, N. J.: Prentice-Hall, 1953.

Bailey, Albert E. B. *The Gospel in Hymns.* New York: Charles Scribner's Sons, 1950.

Berkowitz, Sol; Fontrier, G.; Kraft, L. *A New Approach to Sight Singing.* New York: W. W. Norton & Co., 1960.

Bernard, Harold W. *Adolescent Development in American Culture.* Cleveland: World Publishing Company, 1957.

Brown, Helen A., and Heltman, Harry J. *Choral Readings from the Bible*. Philadelphia: Westminster Press. 1957.
———. *Choral Readings for Fun and Recreation*. Philadelphia: Westminster Press, 1956.

Chase, Alice E. *Famous Paintings: An Introduction to Art for Young People*. New York: Platt and Munk, 1962.

Cole, Luella, and Hall, Irma. *Psychology of Adolescence* (6th ed.). New York: Holt, Rinehart & Winston, 1964.

Crocker, Lionel, and Eich, Louis. *Oral Reading*. Englewood Cliffs, N. J.: Prentice-Hall, 1947.

Dillenberger, Jane. *Style and Content in Christian Art*. Nashville: Abingdon Press, 1965.

Ellinwood, Leonard. *The History of American Church Music*. New York: Morehouse-Barlow, 1953.

Ferguson, George. *Signs and Symbols in Christian Art*. New York: Oxford University Press, 1959.

Gullan, Marjorie. *The Speech Choir*. New York: Harper & Row, 1937.

Haeussler, Armin. *The Story of Our Hymns*. St. Louis: Eden Publishing House, 1952.

Hahn, Elise; Lomas, C.; Hargis, D.; and Vandraegen, D. *Basic Voice Training for Speech*. New York: McGraw-Hill Book Co., 1957.

Hoffland, R. D. *The Ministry to Youth Through Music*. Minneapolis: Augsburg Publishing House, 1956.

Horn, Edward T. *The Christian Year*. Philadelphia: Fortress Press, 1957.

Horrocks, John E. *The Psychology of Adolescence* (2nd ed.). Boston: Houghton Mifflin, 1962.

Humphreys, Louise, and Ross, Jerrold. *Interpreting Music Through Movement*. Englewood Cliffs, N. J.: Prentice-Hall, 1964.

BIBLIOGRAPHY

Hurlock, Elizabeth B. *Adolescent Development.* New York: McGraw-Hill Book Co., 1955.

Ingram, Madeline. *Organizing and Directing Children's Choirs.* Nashville: Abingdon Press, 1959.

Ingram, Madeline, and Rice, William. *Vocal Technique for Children and Youth.* Nashville: Abingdon Press, 1962.

Jersild, Arthur T. *The Psychology of Adolescence* (2nd ed.). New York: The Macmillan Co., 1963.

Julian, John, ed. *A Dictionary of Hymnology.* New York: Dover Publications, 1907.

Keefe, Mildred J. *Choric Interludes.* Magnolia, Mass.: Expression Co., 1942.

Leeder, Joseph A., and Haynie, William. *Music Education in the High School.* Englewood Cliffs, N. J.: Prentice-Hall, 1958.

Lovelace, Austin C. *The Anatomy of Hymnody.* Nashville: Abingdon Press, 1965.

————. *The Youth Choir.* Nashville: Abingdon Press, 1964.

Lovelace, Austin, and Rice, William. *Music and Worship in the Church.* Nashville: Abingdon Press, 1960.

Lowrey, Sard and Johnson, Gertrude. *Interpretative Reading.* New York: Appleton-Century, 1942.

McCutchan, Robert G. *Hymn Tune Names.* Nashville: Abingdon Press, 1957.

McKenzie, Duncan, *Training the Boy's Changing Voice.* New Brunswick, N. J.: Rutgers University Press, 1956.

Marshall, Madeleine. *The Singer's Manual of English Diction.* New York: G. Schirmer, 1953.

Mayer, Frederick D., and Sacher, Jack. *The Changing Voice.* Minneapolis: Augsburg Publishing House, 1965.

Miller, P. J. *Youth Choirs.* New York: Harold Flammer, 1953.

Morsch, Vivian. *The Use of Music in Christian Education.* Philadelphia: Westminster Press, 1956.

Nye, Robert E., and Vernice T. *Music in the Elementary School.* Englewood Cliffs, N. J.: Prentice-Hall, 1963.

Rice, William C. *Basic Principles of Singing.* Nashville: Abingdon Press, 1961.

————. *A Concise History of Church Music.* Nashville: Abingdon Press, 1964.

Rogers, Dorothy. *The Psychology of Adolescence.* New York: Appleton-Century-Crofts, 1962.

Routley, Erik. *The English Carol.* New York: Oxford University Press, 1958.

Shanet, Howard. *Learn to Read Music.* New York: Simon and Schuster, 1955.

Stanley, Douglas. *The Science of Voice.* New York: Carl Fischer, 1939.

Stanley, Douglas, and Maxfield, J. P. *The Voice and Its Production and Reproduction.* New York: Pittman Publishing Corp., 1933.

Sur, William R., and Schuller, Charles F. *Music Education for Teen-agers.* New York: Harper & Row, 1958.

Sydnor, James R. *The Training of Church Choirs.* Nashville: Abingdon Press, 1963.

Thomas, Edith L. *Music in Christian Education.* Nashville: Abingdon Press, 1953.

Thonssen, Lester, and Gilkinson, Howard. *Basic Training in Speech.* Boston: D. C. Heath & Co., 1947.

vonHesse, Elizabeth. *So to Speak.* Philadelphia: J. B. Lippincott Company, 1959.

Wattenberg, William W. *The Adolescent Years.* New York: Harcourt, Brace & World, 1955.

Whittlesey, Federal Lee. *A Comprehensive Program of Church Music.* Philadelphia: Westminster Press, 1957.

Index

123

INDEX